sensational sex

the ultimate guide to sex and passion

Linda Sonntag

hamlyn

sensational sex

the ultimate guide to sex and passion

contents

First published in Great Britain in
2000 by Hamlyn, a division of
Octopus Publishing Group Limited,
2–4 Heron Quays, Docklands,
London, E14 4JP.

Copyright © 2000 Octopus
Publishing Group Limited

ISBN 0 600 60150 1

A CIP catalogue record of this book
is available from the British Library.

Printed in Hong Kong

The author has asserted her moral
rights.

introduction   6

1   sight   8

2   taste   30

3   smell   50

4   touch   60

5   hearing   110

6   raising   126
    sexual
    awareness

index   142

acknowledgements   144

Warning With the prevalence of AIDS and
other sexually transmitted diseases, if you do
not practise safe sex you are risking your
life and your partner's life.

introduction

Real sex is deeply committed sex. This means letting go, and giving and feeling one hundred per cent, in both mind and body. *Sensational Sex* shows you how to raise your sexual awareness on every level, how to communicate it to your partner and experience new highs of emotion and sensation. Focusing in depth on the five senses, it will help you to tune into each one of them, to develop their potential and enjoy them to the full.

The idea behind this book is based on a modern adaptation of the ancient Indian practice of Tantra. The Tantrists are perhaps best remembered for weirdly contorted sexual positions that have no part in present-day life in the West, as they need years of yoga to perfect. But the Tantric philosophy of oneness and wholeness is as relevant today as it was then.

With your mind and all your senses fully attuned to your own and your partner's pleasure, sex becomes not only a physical delight but also a deeply spiritual and healing experience. Developing your sensual awareness will help you unlock your sexual power and transform your life with confidence and joy.

1: sight

It starts with the eyes. One look and we are hooked! Or is there more to love at first sight than that? This chapter analyses the underlying forces governing our attraction to particular individuals, and reveals how we unconsciously send sexual signals to each other by our behaviour and the way we dress. It then explores ways in which we can exploit the sense of sight to enrich our sex lives – the tantalizing thrill of watching without touching.

first impressions

Making judgements

In reality most of us still make the mistake of 'judging a book by its cover'. Fat people are often wrongly assumed to be lazy and to eat vast amounts of food. Thin people, by contrast, are considered to be mean with their food and therefore likely to be mean with money or in their relationships. Fat people are always assumed to be jolly; thin people are thought likely to be morose. Blonde women are seen to be more fun-loving than brunettes, while large-busted women are expected to be more sexy than those with small breasts. Men who are balding have a reputation for being more virile than those with a full head of hair. These are just a few examples of the generalizations that continue to influence our thinking when dealing with others. In this way, we run the risk of limiting our chances of finding happiness.

We only have to stop and consider our past experience with relationships to remind ourselves of the complexity of human interaction. People often say of someone who has let them down in some way, 'I should have followed my gut instinct.' Conversely, many of us will have expressed the sentiment, 'I really didn't like him or her when we first met, but I have been pleasantly surprised on getting to know them better.' Yet in the face of this knowledge, we still rely on snap judgements. However, we would be foolish if, in the interests of being open-minded in our encounters with others, we failed to heed a blatant piece of body language. For example, if someone walked towards us in the street brandishing a knife, we would not stop to weigh up the possibility that they might be on their way home to carve a roast joint. There are times when immediate judgement is called for, but equally there are times when we have more time for assessment. Most social occasions afford this. In these situations, we have a chance to make a judgement and also to review it.

What is it that makes two complete strangers fall in love at first sight; to feel a powerful kind of recognition before they have been given any information about each other or even heard a voice or an opinion? Is it a person's face or their physique? Or is it their clothes, posture or gestures? The answer is all of these, because they all add up to a presence that fits an individual's requirements for a potential partner on both a conscious and a subconscious level.

Most impressions are formed within approximately two minutes of first seeing someone. Using amateur psychology, we collate all the information received, combine it with data already stored in a vast memory bank and come to conclusions about that person very quickly. We slot them into a category according to where we think they stand in the social system. We even assume we know how they will behave or react in different situations. But we can never rely on our ability to make a completely correct assessment. For instance, some of us will have experienced interviews conducted by professional interviewers who have summed up our character and capabilities within a few minutes but not always accurately.

attraction

Sense of attraction

The fact that you can look across a crowded room and be immediately attracted to an individual – a fleeting moment that could change the direction of your life – is both exciting and daunting, but is this just a chance happening? Is it as random as that? How much of what we see is coloured by our own emotional background, unconscious experience and expectations?

A potential mate may have a look about them that reminds us of someone we have loved from afar, or loved and lost; maybe its the way they talk or flick their hair out of their eyes, or their choice of clothes or simply the way they stand. There is something comforting about being in a room of strangers and unexpectedly meeting someone with whom we feel unaccountably familiar. Or it may be that the person you are looking at fits a 'check-list' of desirable attributes in a potential partner that has evolved in your mind over time and through experience. You may also be unconsciously reacting to the positive way others around the stranger are responding.

It is sometimes said that girls choose boys who remind them of their fathers, while boys choose girls similar to their mothers. This is an over-simplification, but it contains an element of truth. We tend to be attracted to people who are familiar to us in some way – perhaps an individual reminiscent of a person who influenced us in our formative years, whether for good or bad. In the latter case, it is a well-documented fact that girls who were abused by their fathers often form relationships, when they grow up, with

men given to abusing women. Albeit self-destructive, their formative knowledge of sexual relationships includes such abuse and it is therefore expected.

Expectations

'Expected' is a key word when it comes to love at first sight. Catching the eye of someone in a crowded room and making our assessment of them involves expecting certain things. Because they look smartly dressed, we may expect them to be polite. Because they have dyed purple and orange hair, we may expect them to be wacky or free-thinkers. If politeness or free-thinking is on our 'check-list' of attraction, when we meet them and have a conversation that destroys these illusions, the initial attraction goes out of the window.

If our preconceptions are upheld when the person who caught our eye comes across to say hello, love has a chance to bloom. Little by little, as a conversation gets underway, we may start to realize that there are many things we have in common, perhaps including absent friends. We may also find that our assessment of their social background or economic standing is correct, and often similar to our own. This is not as surprising as it may first seem. Psychologists and other behavioural scientists tell us that gestures, posture, movements and expressions are learned in childhood, and it is these that we unconsciously sense and on which we base our initial judgement.

14

If we ask someone how they are and they respond with 'Fine!', we are usually able to detect the truth in this reply – even over the telephone. When someone is standing or sitting in front of us, not only does the sound of their reply – happy and positive or hesitant and dejected – confirm or dispute their answer, but our eyes concurrently receive information that may or may not reinforce this impression. Of course, it depends how interested we are in the person concerned. We all know the expression, 'There are none so blind as those who cannot see.'

It is a cliché that eyes are the windows to the soul, but as with all clichés, this one contains a strong element of the truth. Talking to someone in dark glasses for any length of time can be quite disconcerting. Even though only their eyes are covered, it still somehow limits our ability to connect with the person.

We all respond to the way people use their eyes. A person who cannot maintain eye contact could be feeling very shy, nervous or guilty about something, whereas someone who stares is thought to be rude, hostile or even threatening. Yet prolonged eye contact where other body language is overtly open and friendly can be attractive. Eyes that narrow, often combined with a knitting of eyebrows, show anger and displeasure. Eyes opened wide can display enormous pleasure and excitement.

The way eyes reflect character or mood is reinforced by our language. We talk of eyes being shifty, or green with envy, or of wide-eyed innocence, as well as bedroom eyes, making sheep's eyes and giving a glad eye.

Eye allure

Eyes can speak their own language of attraction. Eyes that flit away fleetingly then look back, especially accompanied by a shy flutter of the eyelashes, can be a come-on. A slow blinking of eyes, coupled with a Madonna-like smile, can be sexually intriguing. A wink when given by a woman to a man can be an overtly sexual invitation. However, when given by a man to a woman he does not know, and accompanied by other sexual body language, a wink is often too strong a come-on to be acceptable.

Sexual excitement manifests itself in the eyes in a direct physical response – in the dilation of the pupils. In the 18th century, Italian women would put drops of the plant belladonna in their eyes because it had the property of dilating the pupils, thus making them look sexy. Subdued lighting has the same effect, which is just one of the reasons why candlelight is romantic for lovers.

When we meet someone new, eye contact is the first interaction. We quickly scan their face, usually paying most attention to their eyes and mouth. Should they offer their hand, leaning forward very slightly, giving a firm but not uncomfortable shake, at the same time as tilting their head to one side and smiling with the mouth and eyes, we would probably feel at ease. If on the other hand they took a step backwards, held their head and neck stiffly and simply nodded to us with unblinking eyes and tight lips, most of us would feel very uncomfortable. Their body language is expressing no desire to have any interaction with us at all.

body language

It is estimated that at least 80 per cent of communication is taken up with non-verbal signals. Shakespeare in *Troilus and Cressida* writes:

There's language in her eye, her cheek, her lip,
Nay, her foot speaks; her wanton spirits look out
At every joint and motive of her body.

When two people meet, if things proceed well, their body language reinforces their positive interaction. As they talk – perhaps a little hesitantly at first while they feel their way – they will keep eye contact for increasing periods of time. Their hand gestures will become more expansive and, given time, may even become possessive. For example, a man who is talking to a woman on his left at a dinner table may, as the conversation heats up, twist his body to face her, placing his arm across the table as a barrier to the person on his right.

Similarly, when a newly introduced couple face each other at a bar, there is at first an invisible barrier between them which is gradually broached, perhaps by moving a glass across into the other's personal space. This may be followed by leaning closer or talking more quietly, inviting the other person to move closer to them.

As the attraction grows between former strangers, so the body language becomes more animated. They face each other with wide eyes, eyebrows raised, mouths open and smiling or laughing. Their heads lift back revealing neck and throat. Arms become more relaxed and move away from protecting the upper body. They nod frequently, encouraging the other to continue to talk. The personal space is slowly reduced.

They may even discuss others in the room in a critical way, aligning themselves as a couple. At the same time, they are finding out what it is that makes the other one approve or disapprove. It is the beginning of a learning curve. Later, as the pair have got to know each other and the mood becomes more sensual, quieter more intimate talk begins with touching of hands, an arm around a waist, a kiss on the cheek, and finally, the first kiss on the mouth.

sex signs

When primitive society changed from a nomadic life of gathering fruits and berries to one more dependent on hunting game, the male body developed and evolved to cope with more strenuous requirements.

Modern-day man still reflects these changes. The male body is larger, taller and more muscular than the female. The skull and jaw are stronger to protect against attack. The male shoulders are broad, giving strength and load-bearing ability, and the chest is also broader, with a large lung capacity allowing for physical exertion. The arms and legs are more powerful to assist in carrying heavy loads and to enable faster running speeds. The male body, now as then, is geared to provide for and protect the human species.

The female body has evolved to facilitate child-bearing and is not built for the speed needed for hunting and fighting. The pelvis is wide and tilts back slightly to aid childbirth. Extra fat deposits on hips and thighs with a longer belly give the strength needed for carrying a foetus. Enlarged breasts and nipples have developed for the suckling of the young.

Other differences in male and female sexual characteristics have nothing to do with evolution and past necessities. They are there simply to advertise the gender. The male body is usually hairier than the female's, although loss of head hair often leads to baldness later in life. The male Adam's apple is more prominent and after puberty the voice is deeper. The female body is generally fleshier, with more rounded shoulders, breasts, buttocks and knees.

Gender dressing

At certain times in our history, fashion has accentuated the parts of the body that distinguish one sex from another. For men, the codpiece emphasized the crotch bulge and shoulder pads showed off brawny shoulders, whereas for women, the bustle highlighted the buttocks and corsets trimmed the waist at the same time as making the breasts more prominent. In contrast, during the 1920s, the androgynous dropped waists and flattened breast and buttock line did everything to conceal the female form as women gained an independence previously enjoyed only by men.

Nakedness

The sight of your lover's naked body is an erotic turn-on, and a comfort too. This is because nakedness signifies the stripping away not just of clothes but of all barriers between you, getting down to the simplest truths of your feelings for each other.

The first time you undress in front of each other, desire, curiosity and impatience may be spoiled by a fear of not looking quite right, being too fat, too thin or too something else. Continually bombarded with images of bodies that are marketed as perfect, most of us feel physically inadequate at times. But the body is a house for the person within, and expresses the beauty and desirability of that individual in countless unique ways.

Take time to study the texture of your lover's skin and get to know its various markings, moles and scars. Look at the way the hair grows from their brow. Follow the contours of the shoulders, chest, waist, buttocks and thighs until you know them by heart. Cherish the hands and the feet (take care if they are very ticklish). Wonder at the veins and bones, and marvel at the earlobes and navel. Watch the way your lover moves. Carefully study your partner's genitals through the various stages of arousal.

Most couples take off all their clothes to make love, but sometimes, overtaken by urgency, half-undress may be all you can manage and the more exciting for that. A state of deliberate half-undress about the house as well as in bed can also prove tantalizing. Following Eastern customs, some women like to put on their jewellery for making love. If this appeals to you, bear in mind that in the rough and tumble anything sharp or hard can hurt, and earrings can get caught and pull painfully. For the same reason, it is probably more comfortable to remove your jewellery before you sleep.

Sleeping together in the nude, bodies curled up like spoons or just touching, is a delicious sensation whether you have made love or not, but sometimes after a hot and sweaty session, skin can stick uncomfortably. A thin cotton or silk chemise for one of you smooths things out again without losing the sensation of closeness that can be spoiled by bulky nightwear. When you wake in the night, be sure not to miss the opportunity of studying your lover's sleeping face.

nakedness

Shared nudity need not be reserved for the bedroom. Enjoy the sight of your partner taking a bath or shower and watch the way they soap themselves or wash their hair. The bath is a good place to relax with a drink and talk about what has happened during the day. Instead of putting on fresh clothes, just slip into a dressing gown to eat your evening meal. It is very appealing to see your partner at the table so nearly naked and ready for bed. Or strip off and eat naked in front of the fire, lying on the sofa and feeding each other like the Ancient Greeks and Romans used to do. Plan a naked lunch in a remote wood or moored in a rowing boat, or in a secluded cove – somewhere private where you can swim and make love afterwards with the sun and the air on your skin. Try dancing in the nude, or undressing one another as you go. Try having sex while you dance.

Nudism

Some people find that informal nudity around the house is not enough for them. Nudist camps, where group activities are carried out in the buff, may provide the ideal solution. Some of these pursuits performed naked, such as playing crazy golf or wheeling a trolley round a supermarket, seem bizarre to some but can be appealing and highly enjoyable for others. Nudist colonies are places for families, but if you want to join one, do not try to force your children to take part. Growing children often find their parents' nudity disturbing – how would you feel about your own parents in the nude? Also, do not try to persuade your partner to join in if they feel reticent about public nakedness or uneasy about your motives. To undress or not to undress should always be a personal choice.

Watching

Most of us are turned on by erotic situations. It could be hearing a couple making love on the other side of a wall, or accidentally discovering a pair of lovers in a wood enjoying a sexual encounter. How would you feel if you found your lover masturbating? Would you be shocked, or angry that you were not enough for them? Or would it arouse you? Your response might be a combination of all of these.

It should be said that masturbation, or self-pleasuring, in no way discounts the love and understanding a close couple have for each other. It is more of an extension of that, and it can be an even greater step towards sexual ecstasy if you

are prepared to share it. If either you or your partner are having difficulties in achieving orgasm together, it could be an educational experience – one that will enrich your sexual life thereafter. Watching is one sure way of finding out what makes your lover melt.

Though sex aids hold no interest for many women, some find the insertion of a dildo, or the use of a vibrator, tremendously exciting. A lubricant jelly specially designed for use on the genital area, or an oil such as almond oil, stimulates the labia and clitoris, allowing the fingers to glide with ease, helping to release any initial tension felt by being watched. Alternatively, the use of a blindfold can help you to stay focused and remove any distraction felt by your lover's presence.

or fingers to experiment with different strokes – the middle finger has more strength and control. A hardening and swelling of the clitoris, together with a flush of moist warmth in the vagina, is the beginning of an ecstatic sexual journey. Having found the perfect rhythm for you, maintain it and increase the arousal. At this point, you may enjoy caressing the whole area around the genitals, or the nipples, with your other hand. Some women like to insert a dildo to intensify their orgasm.

Male masturbation

Male masturbation was once considered a sin; something shameful to hide away. It should be seen as a step towards self-acceptance and, in the context of being watched by your lover, a wonderful offering up of your inner secrets. Take your time. Consume yourself in sexual fire.

First run your hands over your body, touching all the parts that you find sensual. Move down slowly, over your belly, and run your fingers through your pubic hair. Slide your hand down your groin and stroke the perineum (the area between the anus and the scrotum), the scrotum and testicles. Massaging the perineum stimulates the prostate into sexual arousal. This move is especially useful if you are someone who needs a longer massage for arousal.

Try sitting with your back against a wall for support so that you can touch these areas more easily. The faster you stroke, and the stronger the pressure on the perineum, the quicker the arousal will be. If the anus is a part of your pleasure, oil it well and insert a finger very gently. Make sure your nails are clean and short, since the lining of the anus is quite fragile. Pay attention to hygiene afterwards.

Lubricate the whole of the genital area, including the penis. Handle the penis gently at first. Holding it with one hand, run the fingers of the other from the base up the shaft, across the ridge to the tip. Move the hand up and down and all around, caressing and pulling. Experiment with different movements and pressure. Pay special attention to the sensitive head of the penis and the frenulum. Spread extra lubricant lightly over the tip if needed and continue your chosen method of stimulation with an insistent rhythm, building up in pressure to the point of orgasm.

Female masturbation

Women may start masturbating later in life than men, but by the time they are ready to masturbate in front of their lover, they have usually discovered the most enjoyable way to reach orgasm. Some women like to lie on their front, others on their back. Some prefer their legs wide open, while others enjoy the increased pressure of their closed thighs.

Whichever position is favoured, glide the hands softly over the belly, move the fingers through the pubic hair and touch the lips of the vagina. Move slowly and purposefully – this is not a race against time. Revel in your womanly beauty. Lubricate the whole of the vulva, opening up the lips like the petals of a flower. When you are ready, use your finger

sex watching

Watching others

Many people get erotic pleasure from watching others have sex as well as from doing it themselves. Women can get just as aroused by sexual images as men, provided they are not intended to degrade or hurt. If looking with your partner at pictures or videos of people making love turns you on, then introduce it as an occasional novelty into your sexual playtime. Use it as a means to more openness between you, to finding out more about each other's daydreams. Often words act as a more potent stimulus to the imagination than images, so you could take it in turns to read each other an erotic bedtime story, or even make up a story that you know will turn on your partner. Mental fantasies are also much more fluid than the celluloid variety, and unfortunately the plots and acting in many blue movies are so unconvincing that they are more likely to cause boredom and snorts of ridicule than excitement. Of course, if you feel pornography violates your sense of privacy, then it is not for you.

Someone who gets kicks from secretly watching other people have sex, but not from doing it themselves, is a voyeur. Other people who do enjoy having sex themselves also like watching couples make love, and this too is a form of voyeurism. In some parts of the world, sex-watching is considered a natural act, particularly in an initiation ceremony. In this context, sex is a public act that is witnessed with pleasure and without embarrassment by other members of the tribe or even of the same family. Still, watching sex is bound to turn making love into a performance and destroy its intimacy. Some people enjoy this and others definitely do not. Make sure you and your partner are both ready for it before you try it, and do not do it if only one of you wants to join in. Involving other people in your sexual partnership, at whatever level, can cause jealousy and insecurities that are hard to eradicate.

Watching yourselves

Many people who would draw the line at watching others gain a lot of pleasure from watching themselves. The advantage of having a large mirror in the bedroom is that you can see what you can normally only feel and imagine. Both of you can watch each other's face and genitals at the same time – something that is usually impossible. It is also a great boost to the confidence to see how radiant you look while making love.

Making love in front of a mirror can be an enlightening spiritual experience. In many cultures, a mirror is a symbol of knowledge and truth, and of purity of the soul. In China, it also signifies harmony and a happy marriage. In Afghanistan and Pakistan, a mirror is used when betrothed couples meet for the first time. The pair enter the room from opposite doors and look at each other in a mirror hung on the far wall. By so doing, it is believed that they will meet as if they were in Paradise, seeing each other's faces corrected and not inverted as in the everyday world.

Of course, some people find it off-putting to have their privacy intruded upon by their own reflections. They say mirrors blow open the intimacy of a bedroom and make it feel more like a shopping mall. As with everything else in sex, you should only do it if you both you and your lover like it, but there is no harm in trying this one out to see.

dressing up for sex

Sexy clothes reveal as much as they conceal about the personality of the wearer as well as their body. Wearing clothes that hug contours and emphasize the figure is one way in which both men and women can send sexual signals. Dressing up for sex in fantasy clothes is something that appeals to people as a way of playing out parts of their personality that they do not normally exercise.

Women usually enjoy wearing clothes that make them feel sexy and get a good response from their partner, but sometimes there might be a niggling fear that the man in your bed is making love to the stockings and suspenders rather than to you. If you do dress up, make sure it is light-hearted and fun for both of you. Fantasies are for playtime only and should not be carried back into everyday life. If a man enjoys the feel of his partner's underwear against his own skin, it is not fair to accuse him at the breakfast table of being a transvestite. All that will do is break his trust and reinforce inhibitions. Similarly, the aggressions and disappointments of your relationship should not be acted out in a fantasy situation, which only requires playing at emotions and needs to be regarded more on the level of a saucy dream. Real anger and violence will shatter the dream and could do serious harm to a partner whom you have deliberately put in a vulnerable position.

Sexy shoes are an essential part of dressing up. Delicate, strappy sandals combined with varnished toenails; exotic evening slippers and mules designed for the boudoir rather than the pavement; red shoes for dancing in; fierce leather thigh boots and stiletto heels all deserve a place in your fantasy wardrobe.

Why is it that many men are turned on by the sight of a woman in high heels? For some, it is because they like the idea of being treated severely by a tall woman in aggressively spiked shoes. It takes them back to a childhood where sexual thrills were associated with punishment. But for most, it is because the heeled shoe gives the female

body a more curvaceous silhouette. To balance against the forward thrust produced by the heel, a woman has to arch her back, which means pushing forward with her belly and breasts. This also has the effect of emphasizing the waist and buttocks. The calf muscle tightens as the heel is raised, creating yet another curve. The teetering walk of a woman on stilettos throws all the body curves into sinuous action and suggests vulnerability as well as sensuality.

There are other aspects to shoes, apart from their heels, that have sexual appeal. The act of pushing the foot into the shoe is in itself a sexual symbol. It is no coincidence that this is how Cinderella was united with her prince. The feet of the ugly sisters were too big for the slipper, and in one version of the story a sister cuts off her big toe in an attempt to make it fit – a clear reference to castration.

The toe of a shoe is a phallic symbol, made obvious in such shoes as the *poulaine*, a male shoe of the Middle Ages with a toe so long it had to be stuffed with moss to keep it erect. It was sometimes curled up and back and chained to the ankle. A modern woman's peep-toe sandal has a similar sexual significance. Shoes and slippers edged with fur or decorated with a fluffy pompon are symbols of the vagina and pubic hair. The fact that Cinderella's vaginal slipper was made incongruously of glass is due to a fault in the transcription of the original manuscript, where it is described not as 'de verre' (of glass) but 'de vair' (of fur), which would have been more symbolically appropriate as well as easier to wear.

Shoes with straps and buckles have obvious connotations of bondage, while shoes that display the arch of a woman's foot or the 'cleavage' of her toes are reminiscent of corsets that both reveal and conceal the breasts.

While few men are serious shoe fetishists, the sexual potency of the shoe works on all of us and is there to be used and enjoyed.

2: taste

Let your passion rip in this chapter, and savour the essence of your partner to the full. Learn how to get the most out of kissing, then graduate to giving your partner an all-over-body mouth massage by licking, sucking, nibbling and blowing. Develop the control and sensitivity of your tongue and lips still further, and sample the ultimate intimate pleasures of oral sex. Feed your desires with aphrodisiacs and sensual foods any time of the day or night, to reach that sublime state of sexual abandon.

kissing

The contact of another's lips as an act of greeting or farewell, friendship, love and sexual desire is a common custom in many societies, though not all. Although Japanese erotic literature as early as the 9th century expounds on the delights of kissing, many Eastern cultures lacked such a custom until it was introduced to them by Westerners. Up to the late 19th century, certain Chinese communities recoiled with horror at mouth-to-mouth kissing, as if witnessing a form of cannibalism.

In primitive societies, where food processors were not an everyday part of the weaning stage, mothers would chew food to make it digestible for their babies and pass the pulp mouth-to-mouth. The young would search with their tongues for the food, so penetrative oral contact associated with love and caring was an early association.

Psychologists and anthropologists who have analysed the act of mouth-to-mouth kissing have theorized that it is a carry-over of the primitive eating habit, involving taking into the self anything that is nourishing and desirable. Modern-day lovers often feel the overwhelming need to consume each other through sucking, kissing, thrusting with the tongue and even biting. The ancient Egyptian word for kiss translates as 'to eat', and indeed the senses involved in kissing are the same ones used when eating – taste, smell and touch. Of these three, taste is the most alluded to in poetry and love songs. As far back as the *Song of Solomon* from the Bible we find: 'Thy lips drip as the honeycomb . . . honey and milk are under thy tongue', as well as: 'And the roof of thy mouth like the best wine . . .'

Kissing, like all other aspects of lovemaking, is something for couples to explore and develop. Given the variety of lip and mouth sizes, it is simply not the case that just because you find each other physically attractive, your mouths will fit together. If they do, it could be a bonus of nature or it might be that one or both of you are great kissers. The art of kissing is something that can be learnt. Violent thrusting of the tongue down the throat, pressing the lips down hard in the misconstrued belief that pressure equals passion, and sloppy, loose wet kisses are all ways not to kiss anyone, let alone begin a potential sexual relationship.

Ways to a sensual mouth

It goes without saying that oral hygiene is very important. Clean teeth and gums and frequent check-ups with a dentist will ensure a foundation for sweet breath. Tobacco stains and the smell of stale tobacco are not pleasant when both partners smoke, but if only one partner puffs and cannot give up, it is doubly important that he or she pays special attention to using mouthwashes and fresh-smelling herbal mouth sweeteners.

Spicy foods, especially garlic, should be given a miss unless you eat them together – particularly in the early flowering of a relationship. Chewing parsley or watercress, or sucking mints, will help in an emergency.

Sensual lips are soft. They can be kept smooth and crack-free with lip balms and creams during extreme weather. Cosmetic companies offer a variety of flavoured lip balms that can add a tantalizing appeal and do not smudge or stain, as some lipsticks can, in the heat of the moment. Check first to ensure that your partner is not averse to the more exotic flavours.

Men with moustaches and/or beards should keep them trimmed – hairs tickling, or worse still, prickling your lover's nose when kissing her can be extremely off-putting. All facial hair should be washed after eating since the smell of stale food can be nauseating. Remember that sporting a beard does not preclude the use of subtle after-shave or men's lotions, although your own clean smell can be just as erotic.

Practice makes perfect

Too often, kissing is neglected in the urgency of a more complete union of the genitals. Yet leisurely kissing can be almost as sexually overwhelming and most tenderly fulfilling. In the past, and still in some present-day cultures where pre-marital sex is frowned upon, or under-age but sexually aware virgin couples resist 'going all the way', hours are spent in sensual kissing, simulating coitus with swollen aroused lips, probing tongues and exchange of oral fluids. Conversely, couples in long-standing relationships, whose intimate feelings have faded but who still need orgasm, will hardly ever kiss during sexual intercourse, highlighting their lost intimacy.

So, kissing can be a pleasurable erotic experience on its own, or highly arousing foreplay, when an increased pulse rate and heavier breathing are a possible prelude to something deeper or simply part of a growing bonding process. But where to begin?

Make sure you are both comfortable. The back-breaking, neck-bending swoop down may look romantic in films but is not sustainable. Start by looking at your partner – really looking at them. You are about to kiss them in a way you would never kiss a passing acquaintance. Cup their face with firm hands. Flutter kisses over the forehead, down the nose and lightly on each eyelid. Ease their body towards you – kissing is heightened with loving caresses. Press your

body kissing

lips softly against theirs and slowly suck first the top then the bottom lip, parting them gently.

Slide your tongue languidly over your own mouth from corner to corner, then repeat the movement across the lips of your partner. Flick your tongue inside their mouth, feeling for the response of theirs. Increase the pressure of thrusting the tongue and lips and vary the kissing techniques in accordance with their response.

Extended body kissing

Just as the lips and mouth send out chemical signals to the genitals, so too can other areas of the body. The skin, with its millions of nerve endings, is a feast of sensuality just waiting to be awakened. Certain parts of the body are always accessible – unless hidden under layers of warm clothing during the winter months. Try kissing the back of your partner's neck, ears and upper arms. The hands too are sensitive areas that are too often overlooked. Feel free to spontaneously reach out for your partner, perhaps in the kitchen or when passing on the stairs. There should be no set rules about the time and place for sexual contact in a warm and sensuous relationship.

When you can, set aside time to spend together. For a mood-setting prelude, try a luxurious bath scented with relaxing or stimulating oils (see Aromatherapy, pages 54–59). Take the telephone off the hook and move into a warm, low-lit room. Candles, either scented or unscented, give enough light and cast deliciously erotic shadows on naked skin. You could burn incense or play soft music that you both find sexually stirring. Place fresh food within easy reach that can be laid on the body and plucked with the lips or licked off with the tongue, without being too intrusive or messy. In short, set a scene that is calming and abandoned.

Run your hands lightly over the area you are about to kiss. The back and buttocks are particularly sensitive. Kiss the back of the neck and work downwards. Make full use of your lips, tongue and nose. Lick and nibble with your mouth and nuzzle gently with your nose. Breathe in your lover's smell. Pay attention and find out by their reaction the parts of their body that are particularly responsive. Avoid those that are obviously ticklish and concentrate on areas not normally touched in day-to-day life – the inner thighs, the backs of the knees, the curve of the stomach. Remember, there are no taboo areas. Both men and women can enjoy having their nipples licked, sucked and kissed. It is up to each of you to explore one another's bodies with tenderness and sensitivity.

Body kissing is a way of connecting with the inner person through intimacy and reverence, and can be rewarding in its own right. But if it is something you both enjoy, body kissing is an ideal precursor to oral sex.

oral sex

Oral sex is possibly the most intimate of all sexual practices. Penetration of the penis into the vagina can be, and sadly often is, achieved without either partner seeing the sacred genitals of the other.

We have already assessed the importance of sight in a potential sexual relationship – probably the first erotic sense. It is usually seeing someone that sets off the first wave of attraction. We see and admire their eyes, their smile and their physique, so why not admire their genitals in a fully integrated sexual encounter? Watching the penis grow or the clitoris flower through the pleasure that you are giving with your mouth is the path to sexual ecstasy for many lovers.

Some people are worried about the open vulnerability of oral sex. For some women, it might seem too gynaecological to be enjoyable, while a few men fear actual injury to the genitals. Oral sex demands complete trust and confidence from both partners. Men especially may fear the penis being bitten inadvertently. Another common fear held by both sexes is that their partner, or they themselves, will not enjoy the sight, taste or smell of this intimacy. There is no reason why, given care and attention, these fears cannot be allayed.

When about to experiment with any aspect of sexual activity that has not arisen before as part of a progressive natural occurrence, there is nothing wrong with discussing it. Sex manuals and educational videos can be very useful in raising discussions about an issue that could enrich both partners' sex life. Men and women can be equally guilty of not asking their partners to try something they want to share because they are worried that it might be seen strange or deviant in some way. Needless to say, this is not the time to pressurize someone into doing something over which they feel they have no control. Any discussion should begin by asking what the other person feels about it. Do they have strong feelings one way or another? If not, would they be prepared to try it out? The aim in all sexual activity should be for both partners to feel confident about giving and receiving pleasure.

As with all aspects of making love, the body should be clean, but this is especially important when it comes to oral sex. The odour of fresh sexual juices can be a turn-on for many, but unwashed stale odours can be offensive. Uncircumcised men should pay particular attention to the area under the foreskin, which can be a breeding place for germs if not regularly sluiced. If either of you has an infection of the mouth, throat or genitals, it is advisable to wait until this has cleared up before having oral sex.

Complete relaxation is necessary for pleasurable oral sex. It should never be undertaken in a hurried or forceful way. Some lovers advocate position 69 (*soixante-neuf*), in which the couple lie head to genitals so that oral sex can be performed simultaneously. Others find the experience so overwhelming that they need to concentrate on their own enjoyment individually.

oral sex

Male stimulation

Fellatio is the technique of exciting the penis by kissing and sucking, and features prevalently in ancient Eastern erotic art and literature. When both partners are relaxed and comfortable, the woman should begin to kiss and caress other parts of the body, slowly and tantalizingly moving towards the target area. Most men enjoy the touching and kissing of the inner thighs just as much as women, and relish the build-up of what is to take place. Caress and kiss the testicles and pubic hair before reaching for the penis. Taking it in one or both hands, lightly slide the tongue along the base to the head of the shaft. Flick the tongue over the top and down the underside, paying especial attention to the highly sensitive penis head and frenulum. Repeat the procedure, but this time use the lips in a gentle kissing or sucking motion.

Slip the tip of the head into the mouth, taking care to guard the teeth with the lips. Suck the head in deeper while caressing the rest of the shaft with sensual movements of the fingers. Suck the head while simultaneously working the tongue around, above and below the ridge. The man should not thrust during this act if the woman has expressed fears of feeling choked, since this could lead her to gag. However, a slow rhythmic rocking to and fro should be acceptable. If in any doubts, the man should remain motionless while the woman moves her head up and down, controlling the depth herself. Alternatively, she can simply use the muscles of the tongue and lips while applying friction to the shaft manually.

Fellatio can be done to the point of ejaculation. However, some women find the idea of semen in the mouth repellent. This can be overcome by stopping in time and bringing your partner to climax by hand or switching to intercourse. However, many women enjoy bringing their man to climax in the mouth and find the taste of the warm fluid delicious. Some even believe semen to have restorative health benefits.

Female stimulation

Cunnilingus, sometimes called *gamahuche*, is the technique performed on women. The man should begin by either caressing and kissing the body from the mouth downwards, or lying below the woman and begin by kissing, licking or nuzzling her legs and inner thighs, using his hands to stroke the outsides of the thighs.

Move the hands across the groin and caress the pubic hair softly. The thighs will part further with increased excitement, revealing the outer and inner lips of the vagina. Working slowly and using fingers if necessary, part the hair and locate the clitoris. Lightly flick the tongue back and forth, in and around the area. Suck the tip gently. If the sheath protecting it is raised, the sensation may be too intense to be bearable. Proceed slowly, perhaps inserting a finger into the vagina to simulate penis penetration. Then, lubricating the clitoral area with saliva, continue lapping with the tongue. Vary speed and position according to her response.

Like the male penis, the female clitoris will engorge and swell as sexual urgency heightens, but the clitoris is more complex – one false move of the tongue in the early stages can put the sexual build-up back to the beginning. If a particular rhythm is working – and this will be obvious – continue to maintain it, unless response dictates otherwise, to the point of orgasm. If the excitement drops a little, caress the body in other places, then return and begin to build up the momentum again.

aphrodisiacs

Aphrodisiacs, named after Aphrodite, the Greek goddess of love, are drugs reputed to excite lust. They may also be taken to stave off exhaustion or heighten pleasure during sex.

In some civilizations, highly nutritious foods were regarded as the most reliable stimulants, and must indeed have had a beneficial effect on the general well-being of people whose diet was usually poor. The Greeks favoured eggs, honey, snails and shellfish such as mussels and crabs. One Arabian recipe from *The Perfumed Garden* recommends a glass of very thick honey, 20 almonds and 100 pine nuts to be taken nightly for three nights on retiring. Other recipes were to be applied externally. In order 'to increase the dimensions of small members and make them splendid', the author of *The Perfumed Garden* advised rubbing the penis with melted fat from the hump of a camel, bruised leeches, asses' members and even hot pitch. These 'rubs' were probably less effective than the treatment of rubbing itself.

The Chinese were more scientific in their approach. They measured and blended the powdered roots of plants, then gave them colourful names such as 'the bald chicken drug'. This drug got its name when a septuagenarian civil servant who took it regularly fathered three sons and paid so much attention to his wife that she could no longer sit or lie down. He was forced to throw the remains of the drug out into the yard, where it was gobbled up by the cockerel. The cock jumped on a hen straight away, and continued mating with her for several days without interruption, all the while pecking at her head to keep his balance, until the chicken was completely bald, whereupon the cockerel fell off. The proud inventor of the drug claimed that if it was taken three times a day for 60 days, a man would easily be able to keep 40 women satisfied.

Another Chinese drug mixed powdered sea grass with extract of liver from a white dog killed during the first moon. Applied three times to the penis and washed off early in the morning with well water, this ointment was claimed to make the organ grow by 7.5 cm (3 inches). As a complementary treatment to increasing the size of the 'jade stalk', the woman could be given a shrinking powder to make her 'cinnabar cleft' a tighter fit. A further Chinese recipe was 'deer horn potion', made of powdered antler, which was designed to prevent impotence.

Horns of all kinds have long been thought to possess aphrodisiac properties, because of their obvious phallic shape, and continuing belief in the potency of rhinoceros horn has brought the single-horned African rhinoceros to the brink of extinction. In fact, the original phallic horn belonged to the mythical unicorn. This horse-like creature was wild, white and wilful, and invariably male. A long horn with a red tip and magical powers protruded from its forehead. The only way to catch a unicorn was for a virgin to sit on the ground near its haunt. The beast would scent her, then lay his head in her lap and fall asleep.

This heavy symbolism has fuelled centuries of demand for aphrodisiacs made of horn, which consists of hard, fibrous tissue similar in structure and content to hair and nails. Like them, rhino horn contains the protein keratin, together with the minerals sulphur, calcium and phosphorus. The addition of these essential elements to a poor diet might improve vigour, but a cheese sandwich would do just as well. The only additional consequence of using powdered rhino horn is to deplete the rhinoceros population still further.

At the other end of the scale from the excitants are the soporifics. These are drugs that induce drowsiness and languor – even euphoria – in which sexual inhibitions melt away. The most commonly used and socially acceptable of these is alcohol. However, alcohol 'provokes the desire but takes away the performance', as Macbeth's porter points out, and the after-effects of too much drink are well known.

On a more everyday theme, eating or drinking huge amounts is not wise if seduction is on your mind. Sharing small portions of delicious food, on the other hand, can be a relaxing and sensual experience – watch your lover peel a fig, or hold a spear of asparagus tantalizingly to the lips.

Cooking a meal together, unless you are both competitive or possessive about your own kitchen, can be an enjoyable way to begin a wonderful evening. Over the next few pages, you will find a selection of recipes specially devised to get you in the mood for love.

food of love

Part of the fun of making an aphrodisiac meal lies in the planning and mutual anticipation of the results. These sexually stimulating dishes should always look good and be served with style, whether eaten on a rug in a wood, in front of the fire, in bed, in the bath or by candlelight at the kitchen table. Let your imagination run wild, outside the normal, everyday rules of preparing and eating meals. For example, the meals do not have to be well-balanced, served with green vegetables or eaten at a particular time. You can drink kir at four in the morning, or snack off a rich dessert for breakfast, if you so choose. The idea is to break out of the mould and do exactly as you like when you like. Eating aphrodisiac foods is part of the pleasure of being free to experiment with sensation.

Hot beef chilli

A robust and energy-giving dish to put fire in your veins. If you like to see your lover sweat, this dish is guaranteed to excite you.

1 fresh green chilli, chopped
1 fresh red chilli, chopped
1 pickled hot chilli, chopped
1 dried red chilli, soaked and cut into pieces
1 small onion, chopped
2 cloves garlic, finely chopped
1 tbsp fresh oregano or marjoram leaves
1 tbsp fresh basil leaves
1 tbsp fresh coriander leaves
1 tsp ground cumin
1 tsp paprika
200 g (7 oz) can chopped tomatoes
1 tbsp olive oil
250 g (8 oz) cubed beef
salt
pepper

Put all the ingredients, except the olive oil and beef, into a blender or food processor and process until smooth.

Heat the oil in a large, heavy-based pan. Add the purée and cook, stirring, for 5 minutes. Add the beef and enough water to cover. Simmer, covered, for about 1 hour, or until the meat is tender and the sauce has thickened and reduced.

Serve with rice, a salad of shredded lettuce and a couple of bottles of ice-cold beer.

Palm beach giant prawns

Hear the sound of the surf and see the palm trees sway in the cooling breeze as you savour this fragrant delicacy from the Pacific. This is a dish to make holiday fantasies come true.

2 tbsp oil
1 onion, finely chopped
2 cloves garlic, finely chopped
8–10 giant prawns, preferably raw, peeled and veins removed
1 sweet red pepper, diced
1 fresh green chilli, chopped
1–2 tomatoes, chopped
2 tbsp fresh oregano or marjoram leaves
1 tbsp chopped chives
200 g (7 oz) long-grain rice
125 ml (4 fl oz) water
2 tbsp white wine
a dash of lime juice
sea salt
pepper

Heat the oil in a large, heavy-based saucepan, add the onion and garlic and fry gently until soft. Add the prawns and stir-fry for 30 seconds. Add the remaining ingredients, bring to the boil and simmer, covered, for 20 minutes, until the rice is tender and the liquid has been absorbed.

Serve with seriously chilled white wine and rippling steel band music. Get the suntan oil ready!

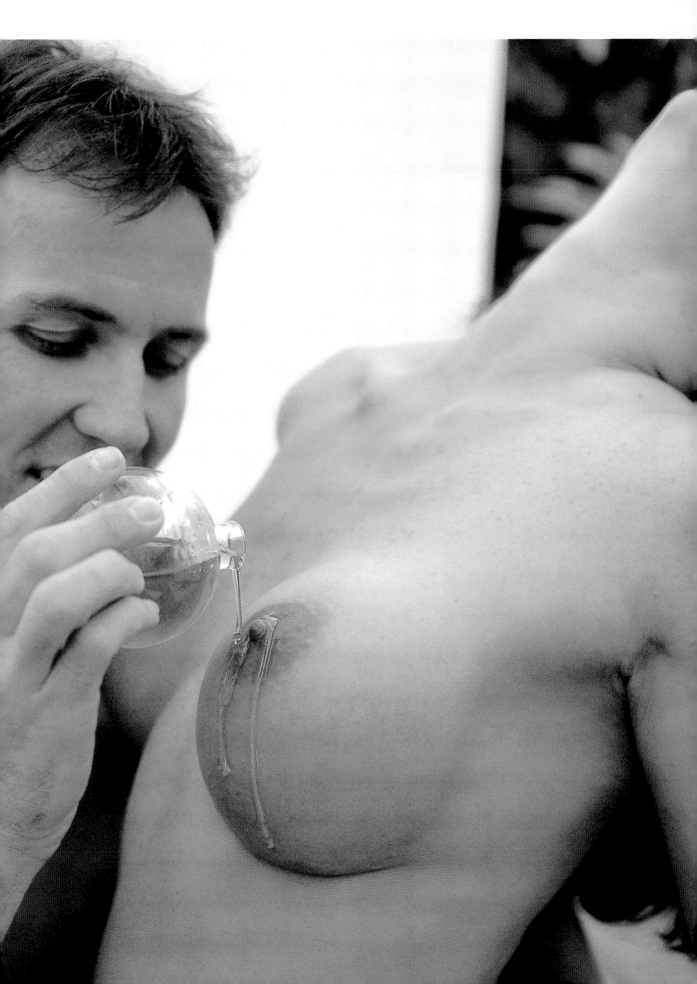

Sole with oysters and ginger

Two well-known aphrodisiacs – slippery, tender oysters with their delicate salty tang and warm, spicy ginger – combine wonderfully in this sophisticated dish.

150 ml (¼ pint) white wine
1 small onion, quartered
1 tbsp finely chopped fresh parsley
1 tbsp fresh thyme leaves
1 cm (½ inch) piece fresh root ginger, grated
2 sole fillets
4–6 oysters, chopped
25 g (1 oz) butter
1 egg yolk, beaten
1 tsp ground ginger
1–2 tbsp lime juice, for sprinkling
sea salt
pepper

Put the wine, onion, herbs and fresh ginger in a saucepan, season with salt and pepper and simmer gently, covered, for about 10 minutes. Add the fish and simmer for a further 6–8 minutes, until tender. Add the oysters just before the end of the cooking time. Carefully lift out the fish and oysters with a slotted spoon and transfer them to heated plates to keep warm while you make the sauce.

Remove the onion from the cooking liquid and discard, then add the butter and heat gently until melted. Remove the pan from the heat and stir in the egg yolk. Return the pan to the heat and heat gently, stirring constantly, until the sauce has thickened. Pour the sauce over the fish, sprinkle with the ground ginger and lime juice and serve immediately with triangles of thin, crisp toast.

Mussels in white wine

The appearance, texture and taste of mussels make them a natural aphrodisiac, and eating them is a really sensual experience. Use your first empty mussel shell as a pair of pincers to pull the next mussel from its shell. Eating with your fingers is always a good prelude to sex.

1 kg (2 lb) mussels, in their shells
small handful parsley sprigs
25 g (1 oz) butter
125 g (4 oz) shallots, finely chopped
200 ml (7 fl oz) dry white wine

Thoroughly scrub the mussels and remove any beards. Discard any open mussels that do not shut when tapped, and any mussels with broken shells.

Chop enough of the parsley to fill 2 tablespoons and set aside. Melt the butter in a wide, heavy-based pan large enough to hold all the mussels at once. Add the shallots and the parsley sprigs. Cover and sweat the shallots for a couple of minutes until they are transparent. Add the wine, and when bubbling, tip in the mussels. Put the lid back on and cook for a couple of minutes, shaking the pan once or twice, until all the mussels are open. Check frequently, since it is important not to overcook this delicate seafood.

Tip the mussels and juice into a large warm bowl and sprinkle with the chopped parsley. Serve with warm French bread to mop up the juices.

For an intimate beach picnic, try this simple cooking method. Arrange the scrubbed mussels tightly packed on a plank of wood, then sprinkle with dry pine needles. Carefully set light to the pine needles with a lighted taper, keeping a safe distance. The resultant flash fire will be enough to cook the mussels.

Stuffed artichokes

Artichokes are a wonderfully sexual food. Both their shape and the method of eating them are highly provocative. Provide small bowls of melted butter. Pull off the leaves one by one, dip the fleshy base into the melted butter and suck it off between your teeth. Scrape out the hairy choke, then eat the stuffing and the tender heart with a teaspoon.

2 globe artichokes
a little olive oil

For the stuffing:
25 g (1 oz) plump Lexia raisins
25 g (1 oz) fine white breadcrumbs
15 g (½ oz) finely grated Parmesan cheese
1 tsp finely chopped fresh parsley
1 clove garlic, finely chopped
melted butter, for binding
salt
pepper

In a bowl, mix together all the ingredients for the stuffing and add enough melted butter to make a stiff paste.

Prepare the artichokes by trimming the stems and cutting off the tough outer leaves. Push your finger into the hole at the top and wiggle it about to make it bigger. You can let your mind run riot while you are doing this! Divide the stuffing between the cavities of the two artichokes.

Sit the artichokes in a small pan into which they fit snugly. Pour the olive oil and a little water into the bottom of the pan. Put on the lid, lining it with greaseproof paper to ensure a tight fit, and set over a low heat. Cook gently, checking from time to time to make sure there is still liquid in the pan, until the base of the artichoke is tender enough to pierce with a skewer.

Lamb with honey and figs

This fragrantly spicy dish offers a taste of the kasbah. Eat this cross-legged on cushions, with a scented candle burning.

2–3 tbsp oil
1 onion, finely chopped
pinch ground ginger
pinch curry powder
pinch grated nutmeg
pinch powdered saffron
375 g (12 oz) lamb shoulder, cubed
1 tsp ground cinnamon
2 tbsp runny honey
4 or 5 fresh figs, sliced
1 tbsp flaked almonds
salt
pepper

Heat the oil in a heavy-based saucepan or flameproof casserole, add the onion and cook gently until it is transparent. Stir in the ginger, curry powder, nutmeg and saffron. Season with salt and pepper. Cook gently, stirring to mix, for 30 seconds. Add the lamb cubes, toss in the sauce and cook for 10–15 minutes, until the meat is browned on all sides. Add enough water to just cover the lamb, cover and simmer for about 30 minutes, stirring occasionally, until the lamb is tender.

Mix the cinnamon with the honey, then stir into the meat and allow to cook for 5 minutes to allow the flavours to mingle. Add the figs and cook for a further 3 minutes. Meanwhile, briefly toast the almonds in a dry pan. Serve the lamb sprinkled with the almonds. Accompany with a fresh salad of bitter green leaves and small, hot pitta breads.

food of love

Pasta with fruit, herbs and flowers

This pasta dish looks glorious and tastes energizingly fresh. The combination of flavours and colours is imaginative and surprising. Vary the ingredients to suit your mood.

4 handfuls dried pasta shapes
I ripe nectarine, sliced
6 ripe strawberries, sliced
8 black olives, pitted
125 g (4 oz) shelled baby broad beans, cooked until tender
50 g (2 oz) feta cheese, cubed
1 tbsp fresh thyme leaves
handful fresh oregano or marjoram, with its flowers, chopped
marigold petals
fruity green olive oil
2 tbsp freshly grated Parmesan cheese
nasturtium flowers, to decorate

Cook the pasta in a saucepan of lightly salted boiling water, according to the packet instructions.

Drain the pasta and tip into a warm serving bowl. Add the remaining ingredients and toss with the cooked pasta. Decorate with the nasturtium flowers before serving.

Risi e bisi

This dish of rice and the youngest, most tender new peas – a favourite of the doges of Venice – was traditionally served to celebrate fertility and its first fruits.

50 g (2 oz) butter
1 small onion, finely chopped
375 g (12 oz) shelled new peas
125 g (4 oz) arborio rice
300 ml (½ pint) simmering vegetable stock
2½ tbsp freshly grated Parmesan cheese

Melt half the butter in a wide, heavy-based pan, add the onion and cook gently until transparent. Add the peas and rice. Cook, stirring, for 1–2 minutes, until the rice grains begin to look opaque. Add the simmering stock a ladleful at a time, then cook, stirring, until it is absorbed before adding the next. Continue adding the stock, cooking and stirring, until the rice is tender. Stir in the remaining butter and Parmesan. Serve at once.

Asparagus soufflé

Asparagus is an obvious aphrodisiac, and eggs are a potent symbol of fertility.

100 g (4 oz) asparagus tips
25 g (1 oz) butter
50 g (2 oz) freshly grated Parmesan cheese
6 medium eggs, separated

For the béchamel sauce:
50 g (2 oz) butter
50 g (2 oz) plain flour
300 ml (½ pint) milk
salt
pepper
about ½ tsp grated nutmeg

Cook the asparagus tips until tender, then roughly chop them.

Melt the butter in a large pan and gently fry the asparagus for about 3 minutes, without colouring, stirring constantly.

Make the béchamel sauce in a separate pan. Heat the butter, add the flour and blend with a wooden spoon. Remove the pan from the heat and add the milk gradually, whisking until smooth. Season with salt, pepper and grated nutmeg to taste. Return to the heat and heat gently, stirring constantly, for 10 minutes, until thickened and cooked through.

Add the sauce to the asparagus and stir in the Parmesan. Beat in the egg yolks one at a time.

Beat the egg whites in a bowl until they form stiff peaks, then fold them into the asparagus mixture. Pour into a buttered 18 cm (7 inch) soufflé dish. Bake a preheated oven at 200°C (400°F), Gas Mark 6 for 20 minutes, then turn up the heat to 230°C (450°F), Gas Mark 8 and continue to cook for a further 10 minutes. Serve immediately.

The imam fainted

The lovely title of this Turkish dish refers to an imam (priest), who, after taking his vow of celibacy, ate aubergines prepared in a special way at the house of a woman so intensely and dramatically attractive that he passed out, or so the story goes. The swelling aubergine with its dark purple skin tells its own story.

1 aubergine, skinned and sliced
3 tbsp olive oil
3–4 tomatoes, peeled
1 fat clove garlic, finely chopped
1 tbsp pine nuts
1 tbsp dry white breadcrumbs
2 tbsp fresh oregano or marjoram leaves
salt
pepper

Fry half the aubergine slices in half the olive oil until soft, then mash them to a pulp them with a fork.

Mix the pulped aubergine with the tomatoes, garlic, pine nuts and breadcrumbs. Season with salt and pepper. Spread this mixture on half of the remaining aubergine slices, and top with the other half, to make aubergine sandwiches.

Arrange the sandwiches in a greased ovenproof dish and brush with the remaining olive oil. Bake in a preheated oven at 200°C (400°F), Gas Mark 6 for 30 minutes. Serve hot or cold, sprinkled with oregano or marjoram leaves.

Lemon syllabub

This is a dessert to eat very, very slowly with small spoons, feeding each other a totally luxurious and sensual experience.

2 unwaxed lemons
1 tbsp muscovado sugar
1 tsp orangeflower water
a few leaves of fresh rosemary, chopped
450 ml (¾ pint) double cream
4 egg yolks, lightly beaten

Finely grate the rind of 1 lemon and set aside. Peel both lemons, removing all the pith, then roughly chop the fruit. In a food processor, blend together the lemon flesh, sugar, orangeflower water and rosemary until smooth.

Gently heat the cream in a heavy-based saucepan over a low heat until warm, then stir in the fruit mixture and the eggs. Cook gently, stirring constantly, for 6–8 minutes, until thick. Pour into a dish and allow to cool. Decorate with the grated lemon rind and chill in the refrigerator.

Strawberry fizz

Something to put on the bedside table, but make it in advance and serve it chilled. You will need a large glass bowl, a ladle, two teaspoons and sundae glasses. Be childish and enjoy it.

1 punnet small strawberries
1–2 tbsp brown sugar
2 glasses brandy
1 bottle sparkling white wine

Put the strawberries in a bowl, sprinkle with the sugar and pour over the brandy. Allow to macerate for several hours. When ready to serve, pour over the chilled sparkling wine. For added eye appeal, drop in ice cubes with brilliant blue borage flowers frozen into them.

food of love

Kir

Kir is made with dry white wine and crème de cassis, a blackcurrant syrup. The charm of this refreshing drink lies in its beautiful, alluring colour as well as its delicious flavour. It was named after Canon Félix Kir (1876–1968), Mayor of Dijon, who is said to have invented it. It is a distinctive drink that deserves a special treatment, so serve it in tall glasses with sugar-frosted rims – dampen the rims, sprinkle with sugar and freeze.

1 tsp crème de cassis
150 ml (¼ pint) chilled champagne or sparkling dry white wine

Measure the crème de cassis into the chilled glass, pour in the champagne and stir until just blended.

Mexican hot chocolate

A rich and luxurious drink for first thing in the morning or last thing at night. Chocolate warms, soothes and stimulates. Definitely an experience where less is more!

25 g (1 oz) unsweetened dark chocolate
a few drops vanilla extract
½ tsp ground cinnamon
2 tbsp thick double cream
2 small cups milk
1 egg yolk
1 tbsp sugar
1 tbsp brandy
2 cinnamon sticks

Combine the chocolate, vanilla extract, cinnamon and cream in a heavy-based saucepan. Heat very gently over a low heat and stir until the chocolate has melted. Add the milk slowly, stirring well. Warm through but do not allow to boil.

Beat together the egg yolk and sugar. Slowly pour part of the chocolate mixture into the egg yolk mixture, and beat well. Add the egg yolk mixture to the saucepan, continuing to beat. Add the brandy and beat until frothy. Serve immediately in small cups with the cinnamon sticks as stirrers.

Orange and lime sorbet

Something tart to make your lips and tongue come alive and tingle.

175 g (6 oz) sugar
250 ml (8 fl oz) water
250 ml (8 fl oz) freshly squeezed orange juice
50 ml (2 fl oz) freshly squeezed lime juice
2 tsp orangeflower water

Boil the sugar and water in a heavy-based saucepan for 5 minutes, allow to cool, then stir in the fruit juices and the orangeflower water. If you have an ice cream maker, follow the manufacturer's instructions for making ice cream. If not, freeze the mixture for 30 minutes, then remove from the freezer and beat lightly, to break down the ice crystals. Return to the freezer and continue to beat the mixture every 30 minutes until completely frozen.

Cardamom coffee

This is coffee with an intriguing kick.

Make filter coffee with equal quantities of ground coffee and whole cardamom seeds. Serve with milk, if you like, and sweeten with sugar or honey.

Tequila

The best thing about tequila is the way you drink it. Sprinkle salt and lemon or lime juice on your arm (or on your partner's arm, or any other part of their body) and lick the pungent mixture before knocking back the drink.

3: smell

Our natural body perfume is a total turn-on. We wash it away, we disguise it with artificial scents, but it is the ultimate chemistry of attraction. This chapter explores the scent of sex – our pheromones and the vital part they play in our sexual encounters. But natural scents other than our own can be used to positive effect in lovemaking. Here, you can learn how to employ the art of aromatherapy to create a seductive atmosphere and induce a state of relaxed arousal.

scent of sex

The scent of sex

Our sense of smell is still a mystery to scientists. We have around ten million olfactory receptors in each nostril, in two patches as big as postage stamps. These receptors are the only nerves in the body directly exposed to the air. The receptors in the left nostril transmit messages to the left (logical) side of the brain, and the ones in the right nostril deliver to the right (intuitive) side. So the smell is identified on the left and described emotively on the right. Smell is the fastest of the five senses – it takes us a mere half second to distinguish which of the 10,000 smells we have logged in our brains is currently being wafted under our nose. But exactly how we do this has not yet been discovered.

The part of the brain that deals with the sense of smell is the limbic area, also called the primitive brain. In primitive times, the sense of smell was far more important and thus better used than it is today. Our distant ancestors needed to rely on smell – the smell of their enemies and the smell of their prey – for survival. Today, our sense of smell still helps us recognize danger, for example something burning or bad food, but is more often used for pleasure, or simply not at all. On our bodies and in our homes, we mask a multitude of subtle, natural smells with a limited range of artificial ones. Also, the functions of the primitive brain, in which smell was so important, have expanded as mankind has

evolved to include emotions, sexual behaviour, cognitive thought, creativity, memory, hunger and thirst and body temperature. This explains why our sense of smell is so intimately involved with all of these things.

Proust's epic novel, *A La Recherche du Temps Perdu* (In Search of Time Past), unfolds from a small and seemingly insignificant incident, when the narrator dips a little cake called a madeleine into a cup of limeflower tea. The delicate aromas that assail his nose send him tumbling back through a vast spiral of memories. We have all experienced similar sensations. If you lost your virginity in a pine forest, the smell of pine would be sexually arousing for ever more.

Pheromones are natural secretions that mark the identity of living creatures. A moth can detect a mate fluttering in a garden miles away. Dogs and foxes follow their noses. Even a snail can find its way home by identifying the trails of other snails. But humans largely ignore the smell of their mates. We use perfume, aftershave and deodorant to disguise our natural sweaty aromas. This is a great pity, because however well suited to someone you feel yourself to be, only the scent of their skin and the smell of their sweat will tell you the truth. If you have ever buried your head in your lover's shirt to recapture their presence, you will know that this is so.

aromatherapy

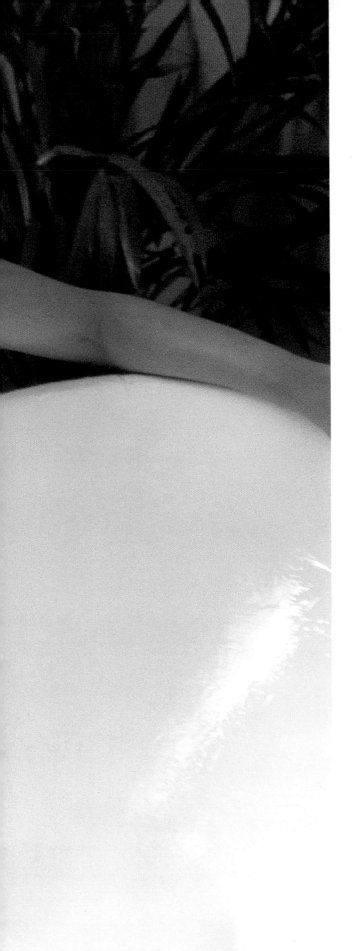

Aromatherapy

Fill the tent . . . with a variety of different perfumes, amber, musk, and all sorts of scents, as rose, orange flowers, jonquils, jasmine, hyacinth, carnation and other plants. This done, have placed there several gold censers filled with green aloes, ambergris and so on. Then fix the hangings so that nothing of these perfumes can escape out of the tent. Then, when you find the vapour strong enough to impregnate water, sit down on your throne, and send for the prophetess to come and see you in the tent, where she will be alone with you. When you are thus together there, and she inhales the perfumes, she will delight in the same, all her bones will be relaxed in a soft repose and finally she will be swooning. When you see her thus far gone, ask her to grant you her favours; she will not hesitate to accord them.

This is an extract from one of the most famous Arab erotic books, *The Perfumed Garden*, which was dedicated to the art of using scents in seduction. The Arabs were pioneers in the art of perfumery. They discovered how to extract potent essential oils from aromatic plants and to take civetone and muskone from the sex glands of live civet cats and musk deer. Today, you can try out seductive scents on your lover at home without cruelty to animals and at very little expense by learning the art of aromatherapy – using the oils of aromatic plants as a complete treatment for physical and mental well-being. These powerful oils can be used for a sensual massage, in the bath and to scent the bedroom with a candle burner.

The practice of aromatherapy is thousands of years old and was probably first employed systematically in China. The ancient Indian medical discipline, the Ayurveda, which is still very much alive today, also uses plant essences to combat infection, soothe inflammation and relieve tension and depression.

It is still not known how essential oils actually work. The volatile molecules of which they are composed dissolve in oil or water. When released into the air, they are inhaled in minute water droplets. At the top of the nose, they are intercepted by the olfactory nerve cells – of which humans have around ten million – and from there their messages are transmitted to the brain. When rubbed into the skin, the aromatic molecules are absorbed into the body through its natural oil or sebum.

Scent seduction

Professional practitioners of aromatherapy design finely balanced treatments specifically for each individual, but for home use, you can select certain oils based on their commonly acknowledged properties. Some are known to lift the spirits, while others calm them. Other oils combine both effects, and these are thought to be particularly good for inducing a state of relaxed arousal. An ideal choice is an aphrodisiac oil which also has medicinal properties beneficial to your lover. Soothing yet stimulating, its rich perfume will bring an extra dimension of pleasure to pampering your partner. Try experimenting with different oils and build up a collection, so that you can choose one to suit your mood and your lover's requirements.

The oils can be administered in several ways, and the treatment is luxurious. But first, the oils must be diluted in a neutral carrier oil. Never apply neat essential oil to the skin, since it could cause severe skin irritation and burning. You can buy oils that are ready-diluted, but if you use the concentrated essence, it needs to be mixed in the proportion of 1:50 with a carrier oil such as almond, apricot, hazelnut, groundnut or safflower oil. Always store essential oils in tightly capped or stoppered dark-glass bottles in a cool place or in the refrigerator. Essential oils are highly volatile, unlike fatty culinary oils, and will evaporate quickly if exposed to heat, light or air.

The diluted oils can be applied to the face and body, and rubbed or massaged into the skin. The base of the spine and the back of the neck are particularly good application points for the relief of tension. You can also inhale directly from the bottle, or add one or two drops to a bowl of just-boiled water, bend your head over it and drape a towel over your head and the bowl to keep in the steam. This is particularly effective when using peppermint, or eucalyptus oil to relieve breathing problems. Another way to enjoy the oils is to add about ten drops to a bath. Make sure the water is at the temperature that suits you both, and share a long, relaxing soak while inhaling the perfume.

You can make ointments and fragrant water with essential oils. For an ointment, melt over heat one part of beeswax with five parts of carrier oil. Stir well to combine, then allow to cool. Stir in ten drops of plant essence and store in a tightly sealed jar in a cool, dark place. Do not add the oil while the mixture is hot or it will evaporate. For a room or body spray, add about five drops of essential oil to 600 ml (1 pint) water. To scent a room, you can also add a few drops of oil to a bowl of water near a radiator, or sprinkle a few drops of oil directly on to a lamp-bulb. You can buy a special fitting for a standard light-bulb which is designed to hold a few drops of essential oil. Candle-burners with a shallow dish set over a candle are also available. Water is poured into the dish, to which you add drops of your favourite oil, then light the candle. The heat vaporizes the oil, dispersing the delicious aroma through the air, releasing a seductive atmosphere into the room.

a guide to the essential oils

Essential oils are wonderful when warmed in an oil burner, the particles diffuse through the air and surround you with delicious aromas. Turn to page 100 for a guide to essential oils for massage.

Basil A warm, peppery smell, evocative of Italian sunshine. Basil lifts the spirits and clears the mind.

Benzoin From the resin of a Malaysian tree, its scent is vanilla. It helps breathing problems.

Bergamot This scent, which comes from the peel of an orange-like fruit, is used to flavour Earl Grey tea. Bergamot fights infection. Do not apply it to the skin before sunbathing or using a sunbed, since it can cause blotchy pigmentation.

Cedarwood A warm, woody, violet smell. This is good for the hair, skin and urinary tract.

Chamomile A warm, aromatic scent, which is relaxing, calming and mildly sedative. This is a good oil for relieving stress and lifting melancholy.

Clary sage A nutty, flowery scent. This gives a real sense of euphoria and is good as an aphrodisiac as well as for menstrual problems and fatigue.

Clove Familiar, warm spicy scent from apple pies and pomanders. Its anaesthetic and antiseptic properties make it effective against pain.

Cypress A fresh, woody smell, which is relaxing and good for the circulation.

Eucalyptus With a characteristic, fresh medicinal tang, eucalyptus is an antiseptic and good for breathing problems. It stimulates the nervous system and clears the head.

Frankincense A spicy, woody aroma from the resin of a tree that grows in Oman. It acts well on the emotions with a relaxing, rejuvenating and uplifting effect. It is an effective aphrodisiac.

Galbanum A hot, pungent smell. Galbanum promotes healing and reduces inflammation.

Geranium A floral scent. Geranium oil is a tonic, sedative and antiseptic, and balances the complexion and relieves anxiety. It also has aphrodisiac properties.

Jasmine A sweet, floral fragrance. Rich, exotic and sensual, jasmine lifts the mood and is used in many classic perfumes. Highly regarded for its aphrodisiac effect.

Juniper A woody, fresh scent. Juniper is stimulating and relaxing, good for stress, fatigue and lack of energy. It is also an aphrodisiac.

Lavender A familiar, clinging floral fragrance. Both a stimulant and a relaxant, lavender is often used for its antiseptic properties, particularly in treating burns. It is also an aphrodisiac.

Lemon A bittersweet, citrus scent. Refreshing and stimulating, lemon is also an antiseptic and astringent.

Lemongrass A lemony aroma. Lemongrass is good against excessive sweating and for migraines, and is also refreshing in the bath.

Marjoram A rich herbal aroma. Comforting and calming, marjoram soothes migraine and relieves insomnia.

Myrrh A camphor-like smell from the resin of a Middle Eastern tree. Myrrh is used in religious ceremonies and for embalming. It is an antiseptic and anti-inflammatory.

Neroli From the flowers of the orange tree, neroli is relaxing and calming. It is good for relieving nervous tension, anxiety and insomnia.

Orange A characteristic warm, citrus scent that is uplifting and refreshing.

Patchouli A seductive, oriental aroma from a tree that grows in Malaysia and the Seychelles. The base of many heavy perfumes, it stimulates in small amounts and acts as a sedative when used more liberally. Patchouli is a well-known aphrodisiac.

Peppermint It invigorates, refreshes, numbs pain and clears the head. Peppermint is good for fatigue, headaches and PMS. It also lifts depression. Peppermint is a powerful oil, so use it sparingly.

Pine A fresh, resinous smell. Pine is refreshing and antiseptic, and good for relieving breathing problems.

Rose A heady, floral scent. Rose is both a tonic and an aphrodisiac. It is beneficial for ageing skin, and improves circulation and breathing. It also helps to relieve headaches.

Rosemary A strong, resinous aroma. Rosemary stimulates the mind and body, and invigorates and refreshes. It is good for fatigue, depression and aches and pains.

Rosewood A spicy and refreshing essence from a tree native to Brazil. Rosewood lifts and enlivens the spirits, and is good used in the bath.

Sandalwood A musky scent. The base of many woody perfumes, sandalwood enhances sexual awareness, acting as both a sedative and a stimulant. It also strengthens the immune system and is good for treating insomnia.

Tangerine A fresh, citrus smell. It promotes zest and energy, and is very good for the skin.

Tea tree A powerful medicinal smell. Tea tree is an antiseptic, excellent for cuts, burns, rashes, itches and any skin infection. It can also be used in a douche to treat thrush.

Thyme A strong yet delicate herbal aroma. Thyme is good for relieving fatigue, anxiety and headaches. A powerful antiseptic, it is used in gargles and to treat skin inflammation.

Ylang ylang An exotic, Far Eastern scent used as a love potion. It is very effective on the emotions as both a stimulant and a sedative. Ylang ylang calms nervous tension and lifts negative moods. It improves hair condition, too.

4: touch

Touch is a simple, eloquent form of communication – affirmative, reassuring, healing, comforting and essential. This chapter shows you how to use touch to express a whole range of feelings in a relationship, from conveying everyday tenderness as a prelude to sexual contact, to exploring different positions for sex, depending on your mood.

Tenderness

In a loving sexual relationship, touch is of vital importance. It is the sense we explore most luxuriously in bed, but the one that is sadly most often missing outside the bedroom. Does touching your partner always lead to sex? Do you avoid touching unless you're going to make love? Or are your bodies are so at ease together that touching is just another way of communicating all sorts of shades of love? Do you snuggle, nuzzle, cuddle, hug, squeeze, push, wrestle, tickle? Are you physical? Are you tender?

In a caring relationship, tenderness can easily melt into sensuality and then to sexuality. But sexuality can always be held in check with a promise to satisfy it later, at a more convenient time. However, many women complain that their partners find touching without sex impossible, embarrassing, even a waste of time.

Why men and women are different

In the days when we all lived in caves, men were the hunters and protectors, and women the nurturers and carers. The emotions that developed to cope with these roles had to be different. Men needed to be hard and aggressive in order to survive. The physical contact they engaged in most was likely to be rough. But women, whose job it was to raise the next generation, couldn't afford not to be tender.

Today male and female roles are not so clearly defined. Modern-day man contributes to the rearing of children far more than his ancestors did. But this change has taken place so recently in the long history of humankind that it hasn't really had time to settle into the male psyche, and make tenderness, touching, caring and listening part of the average male's natural make-up. Most women would claim that inwardly, things haven't changed that much.

Many men are aware that they miss out by not exploring the 'feminine' side of their nature. In most towns and cities there are now men's groups springing up, where men gather to talk on an emotional level instead of competitively, to share problems and get in touch with their feelings. Of course it isn't every man's idea of fun to bare his inner self to his mates. But at least these 'new men' are trying to grow. It's the less communicative types, the ones who just don't express their feelings to anyone, by touch or word, who are most likely to suffer from stress and the illnesses it causes.

The male body, with its strong and powerful frame, was built for action. When primitive man went out hunting for food, danger was constantly in the air. With each crisis, adrenalin pumped round his body and the choice was 'fight-or-flight' – our ancestor had to spring into action to save his skin. In the last few years of his long history on the planet, this same male animal finds himself shackled, perhaps to a desk, or another routine job in which decisions involve small tasks like pressing buttons instead of big actions like attacking or running. But the hormones coursing round his body are the same, and so are the feelings of danger. 'Will I lose my client/the contract/my job?' There is no physical release from the frustrations of the modern workplace. You can't run and hide, and you can't punch the boss. The adrenalin pumps, but the body is forced to sit still, and the consequences can be mental and physical illness.

Men who are not used to expressing their feelings therefore suffer a double disadvantage. At home, their relationship may drift into coolness. At work, they are faced with stress that could build into a life-threatening disease.

Touching is healing

Touch can open up the way to greater self-expression. Massage can bring relief from stress. A loving sexual relationship gives both partners the chance to redress imbalances between them. If it's good in bed, you can make it work out of bed too. Cuddling doesn't have to lead to sex and it doesn't have to be a sign of clinginess. It can express simple comfort, closeness and togetherness.

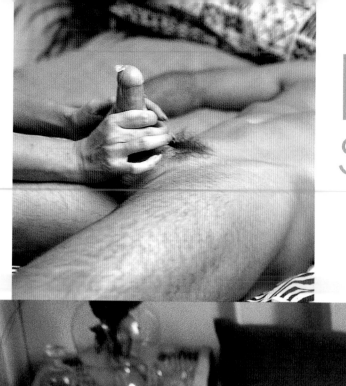

healthy
sex

A fulfilling sexual relationship can help boost good health, but sex and health are also connected in other ways that require serious consideration. The two main areas of concern are contraception and protection against sexually transmitted diseases, especially AIDS.

AIDS is at present an incurable condition that is usually fatal in the long term. It is transmitted by having unprotected sex with someone who is infected with HIV, the AIDS virus. As there are no immediate symptoms of the disease, it is not possible to tell who has already contracted it. This means that unprotected sex with any new partner carries a risk. The most effective way to protect yourself from the HIV virus or AIDS is to use a condom every time you have sex. Some couples who do not wish to use a condom decide to take an AIDS test at a clinic for sexually transmitted diseases to make sure they are both clear of the virus.

How to use a condom

Condoms come ready-rolled and most end in a teat, which catches the semen. To put a condom on:

- Expel the air from the teat at the tip of the condom by squeezing it.
- Place the opening of the condom on the penis head.
- Unroll it down the shaft to fit comfortably.

When fully unrolled, the condom should extend almost to the base of the penis and fit like a second skin, feeling silky and smooth.

After ejaculation, the condom should be removed carefully to prevent spillage. First, the man withdraws his penis from the woman's vagina, holding the condom securely to his penis so as not to leave it behind. Then he removes it and disposes of it. Of course, care must always be taken that any semen left on the penis does not get transferred – on the fingers, for example – to the woman's vagina.

Putting on a condom can be fun. Some women enjoy doing this for their partners. You can use your lips and tongue to help your fingers unroll the condom down the shaft of the penis – but be careful not to snag the delicate material with your nails or jewellery.

sex drive

Understanding our sex drive

Our sexuality is an important part of our individuality and our humanity. The sex drive is a creative force – it creates not only babies, but bonds. Most relationships are initiated by sexual attraction, and while the attraction remains, and sex is good, the bond will deepen. This has a biological as well as a social function, as it makes it more likely that parents will stay together to look after their offspring.

Some people have a stronger sex drive than others. It was once assumed – wrongly – that men thought about and wanted sex more than women. In reality, it varies from one individual to the next, and from relationship to relationship. Someone who has thought of themselves as passive, and not highly sexed, can get a delicious surprise when they meet a new lover with just the right chemistry. But a strong sexual need can arise for reasons other than lust – it can be triggered, for example, by insecurity. If one partner looks like straying, the other can suddenly get very demonstrative in bed. Good sex is always bonding.

How often do you want sex? Some would answer: 'All the time!' Some couples make love at least once a day, even years into their relationship. Others are content with once a week, or even once a month. Remember, this is not a race or a competition. Quality is important, and feelings. Numbers don't matter, but the happiness of you and your partner does.

When the sex drive slackens

When a couple begin a new relationship, their sex drive is on permanent 'go'. As the relationship progresses, especially if they are living together, the sexual needs can still be as urgent but other aspects of the relationship develop. Many people stress the need for affection and companionship as much as full-blown sex. On average, it seems most are quite happy to make love two or three times a week, as long as there is plenty of affection as well.

When a couple have been together for several years, the sex drive may drop considerably. This need not affect the relationship if it is a mutual occurrence. The problems begin when only one partner loses his or her usual libido level. The other partner may feel frustrated, angry, rejected and mistrust their partner's fidelity. He or she may begin to worry about their partner's health or state of mind. There can be a sense of somehow being less attractive and less worthy.

Sex is a part of our lives that can often be taken for granted when going well, but when things go wrong, it looms large and affects every aspect of day-to-day living. Worries of any kind can affect the libido, from the simple immediate worry that you might be discovered by the children to health problems and career and/or financial difficulties.

Loss of libido is sometimes due to physical health problems, such as prostate complications, awaiting or having recently had a hysterectomy, menopausal problems, a bad back or other debilitating illnesses . If physical health problems are not the trouble, there may be a psychological cause.

Events in or outside of the home that may not faze you may severely disable your partner, perhaps rendering them unable to concentrate, get an erection or become lubricated enough. At times like these, communication is crucial.

If stress of some kind cannot be blamed for loss of libido, it could be a simple case of boredom. Sex for one or both of you may have become too much of a routine, following the same menu in the same place at the same time. Think back to the last time you made love. Ask yourself if there was anything different about it from the previous time that you made love. If not, why not? Were you feeling elated afterwards? Were you feeling frustrated? Or was it a 'needed that but glad it's over' kind of response? If the answer to any of these questions bothers you, then perhaps it is time to add a little spice to your love life.

Playful places

Sensual rooms are made for sensual lovemaking. The *Kama Sutra* of Vatsyayana refers to the 'pleasure room', which says it all. If you prefer the comfort and support of a bed, then make your bedroom erotically appealing. Scatter luxurious cushions at the head of the bed – they could be useful for extra support. Use candles, safely dotted around the room, to give that subdued romantic feel. Burn incense or essential oils thought to have aphrodisiac properties, such as sandalwood, patchouli or ylang ylang (see Aromatherapy, pages 54–59).

The sitting room in front of a fire, especially in winter, has all the right ingredients – warmth and romantic firelight. A large, fake fur rug can be a sensory luxury for naked skin. Sofas, particularly those with a drop end, are especially useful for certain positions you might like to experiment with. Soft pornographic videos are a safe way of discovering what each of you find, and perhaps more importantly do not find, a turn-on. They can be watched at the beginning as a form of titillation, or played during your lovemaking as an erotic background. Keeping an open mind and being flexible is the key to enriching your sex life, especially when trying out different positions.

Kitchens, bathrooms, and stairways all have their own place in experimentation. They offer the additional erotic appeal of being normally unconnected with the sexual act and therefore risqué, which can be quite arousing.

Timing

Time waits for no man, it is said, and no woman either. Providing you are sure of privacy, why wait until bedtime? If for whatever reason you feel aroused, communicate this to your partner. In a loving, secure relationship, she or he ought to be able to refuse if the time isn't right without either of you feeling embarrassed or upset. If the timing suits you both, it is a chance to break out of the monotony of routine.

Change your schedule to suit your libido. If you both like to make love in the morning but the mornings are always such a rush, have an early night and wake up earlier. Similarly, if you prefer sex at night but by the time you get to bed you are both too exhausted, go to bed early. There is nothing wrong with going to bed at eight o'clock.

1 Sometimes known in the East as 'split bamboo', this is a delightful way of completing a sensual body massage, or oral sex, in front of the fire.

sex positions

2

The woman lies on top of the man, her whole body
including her legs covering his in a 'mirror image'.
During penetration, she moves herself up and down
stimulating the vulva area at the same time. By closing
her legs inside his spread-eagled legs, or getting him to
close his inside hers, the sensation can be varied. She
can also sit up quite easily from this position, stretching
her legs in front of her, resting on his shoulders.

3

Beanbags and chairs
have more uses than
just as places to sit.
They give the woman
full support while the
man enters her from a
worshipping, kneeling
position.

3

4

As the right height is necessary here, this position offers the pleasurable opportunity to experiment with a variety of furniture in different rooms. The woman lies on her back with her legs wide, while the man enters from a kneeling position. Raising her legs and placing her feet on his shoulders allows the penis to be deeply 'captured'.

5

The woman lies face-down with the man entering from the rear. By placing one or two pillows under her hips the angle of penetration can be increased. From this position, it is easy for the woman to pull herself up on all fours, or they can both roll on to their sides, while still maintaining full sexual congress.

5

6

Described in Hindu erotic literature as 'the deer', this rutting position is ideal for energetic sex. If penetration is too painful for the woman, she can drop down into a more gentle lying position. Some women find its animal-like quality humiliating, whereas others find it highly arousing precisely because of this connotation.

This position is known sometimes as 'lady's will' because, by straddling the man's lap, the woman takes full control of movement and can delay his orgasm if she wants.

7

8

8

Both partners face each other with the woman's legs over the man's to achieve penetration. By leaning backwards into a lying position, genital sensations are more concentrated since the lovers are unable to see each other.

9

Known colloquially as the 'missionary position', this is probably the most popular of all the positions. A couple can hold and kiss each other and gaze into each other's eyes while penetration takes place. It is a relaxing way, particularly for the man, to achieve orgasm after other more athletic positions have been shared.

10

In fellatio, the partner uses the lips and
tongue to kiss, caress, suck and lick the
penis. It is perhaps the most intimate way a
woman can express her desire and love for
the most masculine part of the male body,
known in the *Kama Sutra* as the 'lingam'.

sex positions

One of the most exquisite ways of achieving female orgasm is through the gentle art of cunnilingus. The wet softness of the lips and tongue are used to stimulate the clitoris in a variety of luscious ways.

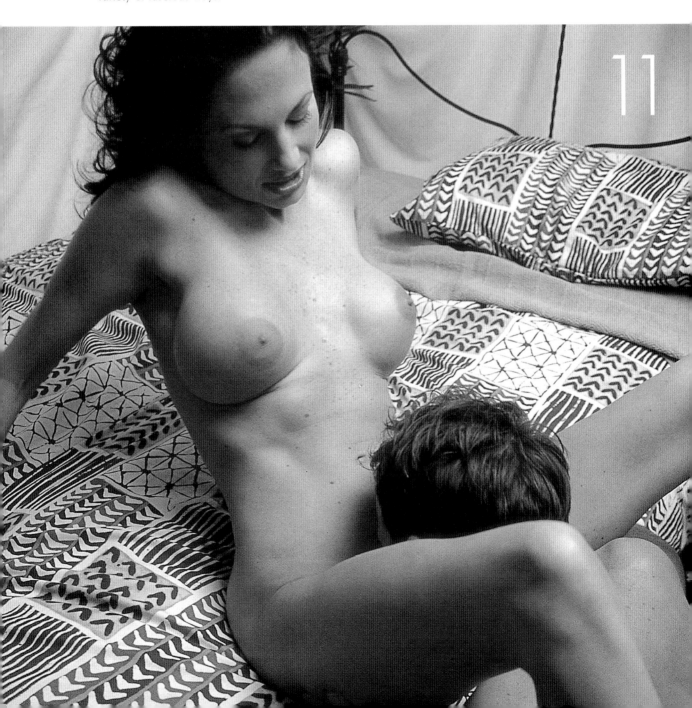

12

A strenuous position that demands great neck, arm and leg strength on the part of the man. The woman holds on tightly while moving herself up and down. For the physically fit, it is a fun way to begin penetration before being lowered on to a table or a bed.

13

Known as the 'cuissade' from the French *cuisse*, meaning thigh, this is a half rear-entry position which still enables a couple to gaze upon each other and kiss face to face. The woman rests her raised leg on the man's body, while he enters 'secretly' from under her thigh.

13

14
Known in the *Kama Sutra* as the 'yawning position', the woman lies on her back, resting her legs on the man's shoulders. Raising the woman's buttocks with the use of cushions increases the depth of penetration. Another variation in the *Kama Sutra* is the 'pressing position'. This involves lowering the legs and bending them in front of the man's chest.

15
Use the support of a wall or firmly closed door when an urgent need for each other becomes overwhelming. Penetration is achieved by the woman raising a leg coquettishly around the man.

15

16

This position is known in China and Japan as 'mandarin ducks', in India as the 'cobra' and in the West as 'spoons'. It has long been popular with partners whose physical weight creates problems, and is also useful during pregnancy. Both partners lie on their sides with the man entering from the rear.

17

In this position, the woman is definitely in control. Some men like the idea of being 'taken' while they remain helpless with their hands tied. A blindfold can add a little to the game, as the loss of sight tends to heighten the sense of touch.

sex positions

18

After washing each other in a cosy bathroom, what could be more natural than fast, steamy sex? By thrusting against one another, sexual momentum builds up to a crescendo.

19

A half-way position that can begin the sexual sequence or facilitate a change from one position to another, without breaking contact. Here, the woman can deepen the man's thrust by folding her leg around him, drawing him even closer.

19

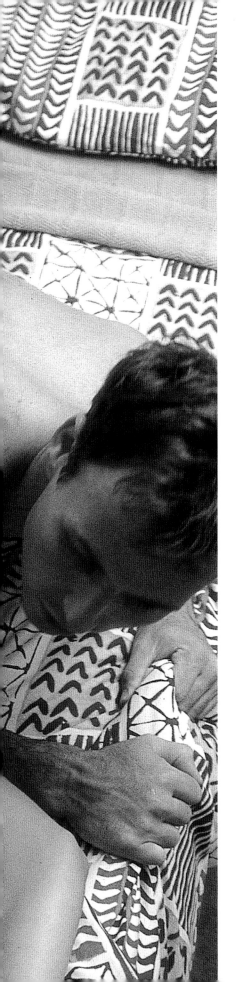

20

The man lies diagonally across the woman, as he penetrates her. Gentle rocking from side to side builds up a delicious sexual rhythm.

21

The woman lies on her back and the man sits astride her, facing her feet. She reaches forward to masturbate him, while he masturbates her. Because neither partner can see the other's face, this position offers total concentration on sensation alone. Before starting, the man may enjoy inserting 'love eggs' in the vagina to give the woman extra sensation.

21

shiatsu

Shiatsu

Shiatsu is a Japanese therapy based on a traditional form of massage. Like other Oriental healing methods, its roots lie in the philosophy and medical theory of acupuncture. Literally translated, *shiatsu* means finger pressure, but practitioners also use the palms of their hands and sometimes their elbows, knees and feet to apply stronger pressure. In addition, they employ stretching exercises to increase the subject's suppleness and flexibility.

Shiatsu works with the flow of energy (called *ki* or *chi*) that runs through the body in channels known as meridians. By working pressure points (called *tsubos*) along these meridians, blockages are dissolved and the flow of energy is released. Shiatsu can be used as a tool for healing and as preventative medicine to promote general wellbeing.

Shiatsu practitioners can diagnose and treat specific problems during a session that works over the whole body. The treatment does not hurt, though surprisingly sore or tender areas may be uncovered that reveal weak spots in your physical or emotional health. You may feel very relaxed or sleepy after shiatsu and later on elated and energetic, and generally very positive about the world.

It takes years to train as a shiatsu practitioner, and qualifying standards are rigorous, but anyone can learn a basic sequence for use at home, so you can treat yourself as well as your partner.

shiatsu

Shiatsu for good sex

Sexuality is governed by the kidney meridian. The kidneys provide life energy for all the other organs, as well as for reproduction, birth and growth. They also nourish the spine, bones and brain and generate dynamism and willpower.

The kidney pressure points, or *tsubos*, are located about two finger-widths either side of the spine, level with the space between the second and third lumbar vertebrae. Both *tsubos* should be worked. Treatment of these *tsubos* is used for infertility as well as lack of sexual energy. It also strengthens the body and recharges the will, relieving exhaustion, depression, chronic lower back pain, chronic ear problems, such as tinnitus and deafness, and poor vision.

How do you know if you have found the right place? You may feel that your finger or thumb nestles comfortably into a small hollow that you sense is the spot, or you may just feel intuitively that you have located it.

Once you have found the right spot, you can learn to diagnose the state of energy in the *tsubo*. It may feel full of energy, with strong muscle tone or a sharp tender feeling the Japanese call *jitsu*. In this case, energy needs to be dispersed. You can simply keep your finger or thumb on the spot, or make small circular motions with it, or a repeated pumping action until you feel the energy relax. If the energy is lacking, on the other hand, the *tsubo* will feel soft and yielding, or needy. Bring energy back into an empty spot by simply holding the point until you feel energy and muscle tone return.

Always exert pressure at right angles to the surface of the skin so that you reach deep into the *tsubo*. If the angle is out, the treatment will be far less effective.

Other points to try

For lack of sexual energy in men or abnormal menstruation, pressing a point called the 'greater stream' could help. This is found midway between the tip of the ankle bone and the Achilles tendon.

For menstrual pain, try the aptly named 'ocean of blood', which is found four finger-widths above the kneecap on the bulge of the muscle.

Also for menstrual pain and female reproductive problems, press the 'meeting point' of the three 'yin leg meridians', which you will find at four finger-widths above the tip of the ankle bone. Push in to the edge of the tibia.

Another point that treats reproductive problems as well as fatigue is the 'gate to the original chi', which is found in the centre of the body, four finger-widths below the navel.

Pressure to the 'heavenly pivot', located two thumb-widths either side of the navel, helps to relieve menstrual pain.

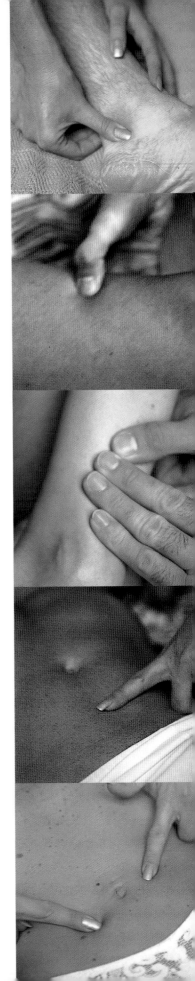

reflexology

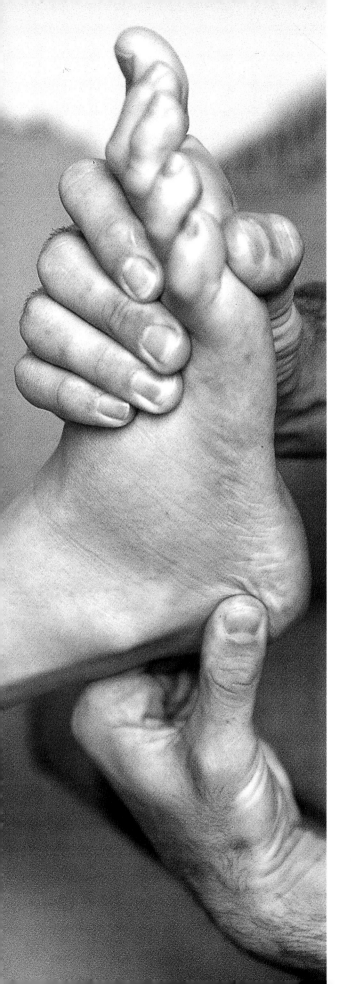

Reflexology

Reflexology is a therapy that involves massage to reflex points on the feet, or sometimes on the hands. Its aim is to trigger healing by unblocking the flow of energy in corresponding parts of the body.

The origins of reflexology date back 5,000 years to ancient China, where a form of pressure therapy to the feet was commonly practised. Similar techniques were known in ancient Egypt, and tomb drawings show feet being held and massaged. In more recent times, foot reflexology was practised by Native American peoples and in Africa. However, it was an American physician, Dr William H. Fitzgerald, who in the early 1900s began systematically to divide the feet into zones and to specify the area of each foot that corresponds to each body part and internal organ.

He drew a zonal map of the body, dividing it into five zones on each side, running up from the toes to the head, and from the fingers to the head. The zones from the toes and fingers intersect each other at the neck. Dr Fitzgerald's assistant, Dr Edwin Bowers, demonstrated how the zone theory works in a startling way. He applied pressure to an area of a colleague's hand or foot, then stuck a pin in the corresponding area of the face anaesthetized by the pressure – obviously not something you should try at home. This experiment was a graphic demonstration of how pain in one part of the body could be relieved by pressure on a corresponding point in the hand or foot.

Dr Fitzgerald explained that tension, infection, inflammation or congestion in the body will affect the entire zone in which the problem lies. If the area remains blocked, the problem will spread to the zones on either side. But a reflexologist can tell the source of the trouble by the patient's sensitive reaction when the corresponding part of the foot is pressed, and therapeutic pressure to that part will unblock the entire zone. However, you do not need to wait for a problem to arise to enjoy the benefits of reflexology.

With a little time and practice, you can learn some of the techniques of reflexology and then apply them to your own or your partner's feet. Those presented here focus on specific points for treating the uterus and prostate, and the ovaries and testicles. Try them out on each other and see if they stimulate your sex drive.

95

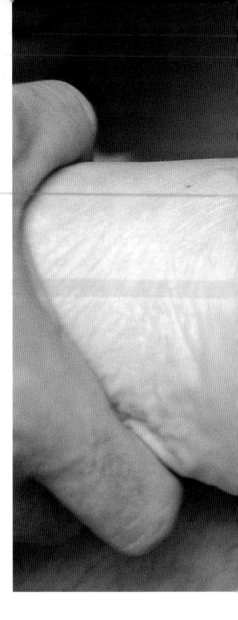

reflexology

Reflex point for the uterus and prostate

This reflex point is found on the inside of the foot below the ankle bone. This area of the foot is usually tender, so sensitivity here is quite normal. Working the area can have a beneficial effect on allergic reactions as well as stimulating the sex drive.

To find the reflex point, put the tip of your index finger on the ankle bone and the tip of your little finger on the back corner of the heel, as shown. Place the tip of your middle finger on the point midway between them. This is the point to be worked.

Use your right hand to work the area on the left foot. Cup the heel in your right hand and place the tip of your middle finger on the pressure point. Hold the top of the foot with your right hand. With your right hand, rotate the foot several times, first one way and then the other. Try increasing the pressure of your middle finger, but lessen it if it gets uncomfortable. Working the point by rotating the foot enables you to pinpoint the exact place without undue discomfort to your partner.

Now repeat the technique, reversing hands, on the other foot.

Reflex point for the ovaries and testicles

This is on the opposite side (outside) of the foot. To find it, use the same technique as before. Since this side of the foot is less sensitive, you can work the point with your thumb, exerting pressure with a small circulating movement.

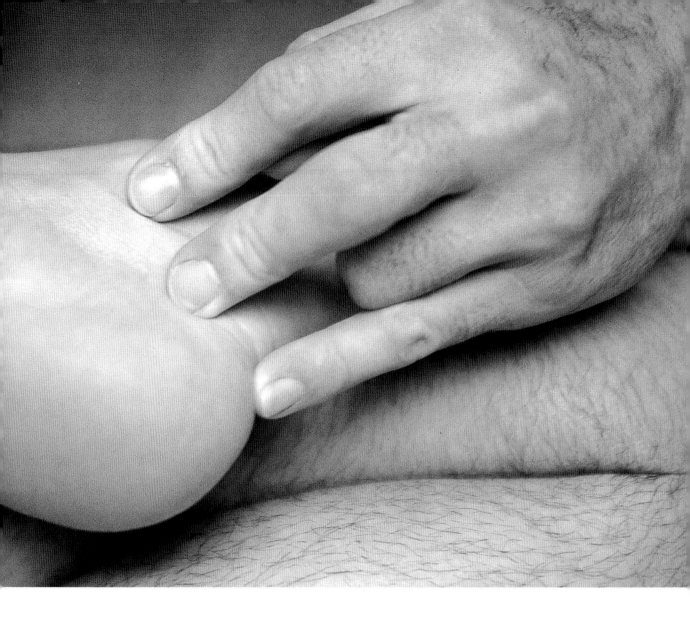

massage

Massage

In most Western cultures, massage is still thought of as being 'alternative'. Yet massage is the norm in the many societies that have a holistic philosophy of life – mind, body and spirit all acting as one. In such communities, touch is the essence of life. In Morocco, new-born babies and their mothers are massaged with herbal remedies to promote health and aid recovery. In India, it is routine for mothers to massage their offspring and pass on this knowledge to their children. In Ancient Greece, Hippocrates, the reputed founder of medicine, recommended a daily bath and massage with essential oils to promote good health.

In the West, we start off life experiencing touch in the womb, being massaged by the amniotic fluid and gently bumping into our mother. During the first few months, particularly when being breastfed, we are constantly being cuddled and touched. As toddlers in a loving family we continue to be petted and fondled, but as we grow, touch becomes less important.

Beneficial effects

Psychologists have long been researching the beneficial effects of massage. It has also been scientifically proven that tactile stimulation of a pleasurable kind releases hormones – endorphins – which promote a sense of wellbeing and aid recovery from illness.

Massage relieves stress and muscle tension. It is a powerful overall mind and body therapy. If being massaged by a qualified practitioner can do all this, think about the mind-blowing possibilities of being massaged by a lover – someone who knows your body intimately who can touch parts others cannot reach? Maybe you have a new lover who is longing for the chance to explore, worship and provide sexual healing.

Preparations for massage are simple, but should be carried out with careful thought.

Location

The bedroom is the ideal place for massage, but most modern beds are too soft. The Japanese futon is perfect, but the floor is a good substitute. Use a folded blanket for cushioning, covered with a large absorbent towel. The room should be warm and softly lit. Candlelight is an added bonus. Candles can be scented or used in conjunction with burning incense or fragrant essential oils to give an exotic atmosphere if this appeals (see Aromatherapy, pages 54–59). Music, especially New Age compilations, recorded to play for a long time without drama or interruption, are ideal for setting a tranquil mood. Ensure that you have complete privacy and unplug the telephone, unless you have an answermachine that does not boom the caller's voice across the room.

Requirements

Extra towels may be needed for covering parts of the body not being massaged, to maintain body temperature. It is surprising how quickly the body loses excess heat, especially when relaxed.

Oil allows the hands to glide over the skin without friction. Ordinary vegetable oil is perfectly adequate, but you will find more luxurious massage oils in most major pharmacies. Both of these can be used on their own or have the addition of a few drops of an essential oil. Essential oils have been used for at least 5,000 years. The oldest known distillery is in the Indus Valley in South Asia.

When added to a carrier oil and used in massage, essential oils give an extra boost to stimulation and relaxation, with many offering aphrodisiac properties. A chart on page 101 lists some of the oils recommended for massage. Never apply essential oils directly to the skin, since they can cause severe irritation and burning.

essential oils for massage

Essential oils must be used with care. Never increase the recommended amounts, since this could have a reverse effect or even be toxic. It is advisable to carry out a skin test prior to using any essential oil, since not all oils agree with everyone. Oils should not be used in the first three months of pregnancy, and only used in the later months after consulting a doctor.

Preparations for massage

A luxurious bath is always preferable before a massage. Try sharing and washing each other, but keep arousal under control. This will increase anticipation of what might become a full-blown sexual conclusion to the massage.

Place oils in a safe place close by where they won't be knocked over. Before applying to the body, always warm in your hands first. Cold oil is never sensual.

Make sure your lover is lying face down in a relaxed position. Before you begin, centre yourself. Create a space to allow the energy, or sacred breath of life (yogis call this *prana*), to flow through the body into the fingertips. Breathe in deeply through the nose. Hold your breath for a few seconds, then exhale through the mouth. Try to exhale for double the time of the inhalation. Do this three times, but no longer – if you are unused to yogi breathing, it could make you dizzy. Try to put all mundane and irritating thoughts out of your mind.

Relax the hands and wrists by shaking them. Kneel by your lover's side and, with a straight back, move from the pelvis and begin the massage.

Massage strokes

There are several different types of strokes used in massage. Tapotement, or the 'chopping' and 'striking' of the body with the hands, is perhaps what most people think of first, but for a sensual massage, use the following three:

Effleurage is a long flowing stroke, useful when applying oil. The hands stroke the body slowly and gently with an even pressure. It is a relaxing way to begin a massage.

Petrissage, or skin rolling, is a rhythmic pulling up of the skin and squeezing. Contrary to its description, it can be very sensual if done properly.

Kneading is used to apply friction with the palms of the hands. It is especially good for relaxing the limb muscles. The thumbs and fingers are used to concentrate on smaller areas of knotted tension.

Type	Uses and Properties	Method
Relaxing oils		
Rose	Emotional soother Good for dry, sensitive skin Aphrodisiac	Body & facial massage In bath
Lavender	Soporific Good for most skin types	Body & facial massage In bath
Camomile	Good for dry, sensitive skins Soothing	Body & facial massage In bath
Ylang ylang	Emotional soother Softens skin Aphrodisiac Safety note: dilute well	Body massage In bath
Neroli	Stress-buster Skin conditioner	Body & facial massage
Rosemary	Nerve-soother	In bath
Stimulating oils		
Frankincense	Aphrodisiac	Body massage In bath
Patchouli	Conditions skin Aphrodisiac	Body massage In bath
Geranium	Aphrodisiac Good for oily skins Safety note: avoid sensitive skin	Body & facial massage In bath
Juniper berry	Anti-tiredness Promotes well-being	Body & scalp massage In bath
Bergamot	Cooling in hot weather Safety note: avoid sensitive skin	Body & facial massage In bath
Cedarwood	Soothing for itchy skin Aphrodisiac	Body & facial massage In bath
Cinnamon	Stimulating Aphrodisiac Safety note: dilute well	Body massage

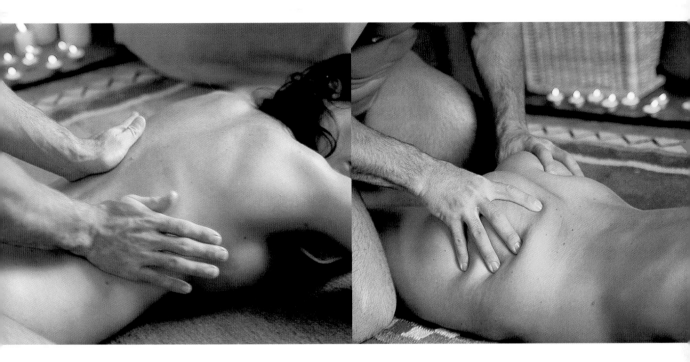

Massaging the back

Begin to apply the oil. Use the effleurage technique, massaging from the lower back either side of the spine towards the shoulders. Push your hands in one sensual movement, following the natural contours. Lean forwards as the hands move further up.

Move both hands outwards across each shoulder, then using your fingers, lightly slide down to rest in the starting position. Repeat this several times, moving further away from the spine towards the sides each time.

Increase the pressure with a kneading rhythm. Use the heel of the hands as you caress upwards and give a light, smooth sweep back to the base of the spine with the flat of the hand. Rotate your finger and thumb pads on spots that feel knotty.

Massaging the buttocks

Begin at the top of the buttocks with fingertips touching and elbows pointing outwards. Move down firmly, kneading deeply with the palms. Follow the contours of the buttock sides, fanning out the hands so that the wrists meet at the base of the cheeks. Hold the cheeks together.

Begin moving upwards with a firm pressure, reversing the hand movements so that they meet at the starting point with the fingertips together again. This has a sensual effect on the genitals.

Finish with an effleurage movement up to the neck and back down again.

Massaging arms and hands

Begin by using long, voluptuous strokes from the shoulder to the hand.

Hold the hand and gently tug the fingers and thumb, one by one. Slide your ring and middle finger either side of each of your partner's fingers. Turn the palm up and massage with the thumb in a circular motion.

Circle your hand around the arm, repeating a squeeze-and-move-upwards movement. Smooth the flat of the hand down from the shoulder to the wrist. Repeat several times.

Using petrissage, work up the arm smoothly. Brush down towards the wrist with feathery strokes. Knead all the way to the shoulder, using the thumbs. Repeat several times. Enclose the arm in both hands and slide the hands down slowly, ending with the fingertips.

Massaging the chest and abdomen

Begin with firm effleurage circular strokes, working across the whole chest.

Using the heels of the hands, knead the upper chest on both sides.

Repeat effleurage strokes across the chest, then up, over and under the shoulders. Massage the underside of the shoulders with the thumbs. Draw the fingers towards you, picking up and squeezing the muscles gently but firmly. Finish with long, light strokes across the shoulders and down the chest.

Massaging the legs and feet

Using the heel of the hand, knead the arch firmly towards the heel. Return to the ball with a single firm stroke. Repeat several times.

Circle the thumbs firmly from the heel to the toes. Rotate the ankle carefully in both directions.

Place your hands either side of the ankle. Massage using a circular kneading movement with the fingers.

Flex toes back and forth very gently. Finally, rotate and pull each toe individually. Slide them sensually between your fingers and let them drop loose.

Using deep effleurage strokes, move upwards to the groin. Return to the starting point, caressing the inner leg gently. Repeat the movement, but this time up the sides of the leg.

Knead the upper surface of the thigh firmly with the thumbs. Use the heel of one hand to knead the sides while countering the pressure by holding the leg still with the other. Repeat the movement, concentrating on the back of the thigh. The leg will have to be raised slightly as you work upwards – one hand on the top, the other underneath.

Using petrissage, work from the inner thigh, over the top surface to the outer thigh.

Alternately knead then pick up and roll the calf muscles with the thumbs and fingers. Finally, smooth the flats of the hands seductively down from the thigh top to the toes.

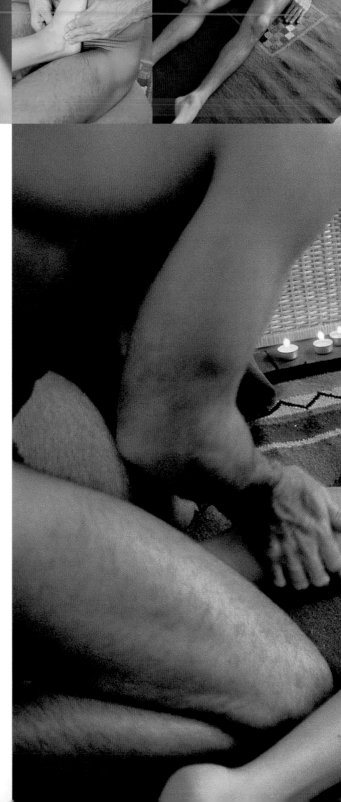

massage

Aquatherapy

Throughout history, bathing has been associated with many anecdotes and myths, Cleopatra reputedly bathed in asses' milk. Early Christians believed that washing was a pagan invention and therefore ungodly. Communal bath houses were built as far back as Roman times, but the idea of every house having a bathroom is a relatively modern concept.

Where would we be without a bathroom? There is nothing as relaxing as soaking away the aches and strains of our hectic lives or starting the day with an invigorating shower, except perhaps to share this recreation with a lover.

As a prelude to making love, sharing a bath or shower is delectable. It not only ensures that both partners feel beautifully fresh, but is also a bonding process. In the animal kingdom, mutual grooming is an intimacy that reinforces relationships, something that can certainly be applied to human lovers. Soapy hands gliding all over your own or your lover's skin are a slow and delicious titillation – one of the most amorous and caring kinds of foreplay.

Add a few drops of your favourite aromatherapy oil to the bath water and soon the bathroom will be filled with an erotic scent that cannot fail to heighten the bathtime sensual experience. Try ylang ylang, sandalwood or patchouli for a particularly heady aroma.

Using a loofah to exfoliate the dead skin, followed by a cool shower, will leave you both tingling and glowing. Wash each other's hair with a scalp-stimulating shampoo such as rosemary. Use the fingertips in a circular motion to massage the scalp from the back of the neck up to the forehead and down at both sides, then rinse thoroughly.

Match your exotically scented bodies with a little erotic play using the shower. Powerful jets of water can be a boon to tired and aching muscles, but they can also have the added bonus of sexually stimulating the nipples, clitoris and penis. Make sure that the water force and temperature is comfortable and never forcefully squirt inside the vagina. This could be harmful. Experiment with the direction of the shower nozzle and discover what makes your lover quiver with pleasure.

Complete your pampering by smoothing on moisturizing cream and wrapping each other up in warm, fluffy towels.

5: hearing

The ear is an instrument of balance, finely attuned to harmony and discord. Talking in bed offers the opportunity to tell your partner how you really feel and what you want, to share confidences as well as fantasies. But equally as important as the need to talk is the ability to listen and understand. We speak the same language – or do we? Men and women express themselves differently. This chapter explains how to increase understanding and communicate more effectively.

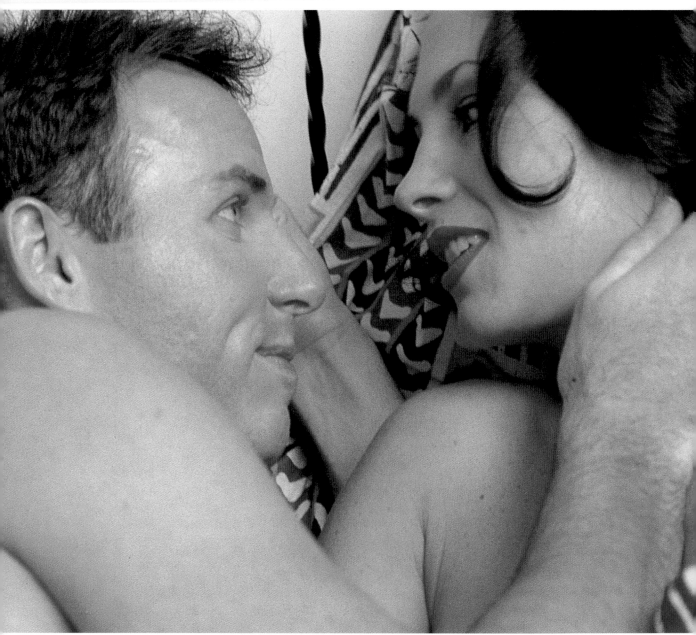

talking

Talking in bed

Bed can be the best place of all to talk. It is a sanctuary and a refuge, your private nest where you go to recuperate and relax. Thoughts drift into your head and you can say just what you are feeling into a companionable and sleepy silence. The pressure for a structured conversation has gone. The need to organize and be practical has slipped away with the end of the day.

Sometimes it is good to go to bed early just to talk. Have a bath together. Then wrap yourselves in big towels and take a drink to sip under the duvet. Propped up comfortably on pillows side by side, your bodies parallel, perhaps with a window or a favourite picture at the end of your bed to lose yourself in, you have more space to delve into your own thoughts than when sitting face to face. As when you are on a walk together, it is a good time for catching up with what has been happening and laughing over shared memories, as well as for dreaming and planning.

Bed is a place for trust. It is not the place to make major revelations that will upset or wound your partner. Neither is it the place for starting a row. But it is the place for making up once the row is over, and turning the passion of anger into sex.

Talking through problems

Bed can also be the place for talking calmly together about difficult things, lying and looking into one another's eyes. It is certainly the place for helping each other with emotional and sexual problems. Because men can find it more difficult to talk about love and sex, it usually falls to the woman to take the lead. Keep it simple, keep it honest and avoid criticism, blame, recriminations, comparisons – anything that might wound. Try to break through your partner's inhibitions by talking first about your own feelings, fears and inadequacies. Aim to spend as much time listening as talking. Men sometimes need time to become convinced that you will not think less of them for admitting to emotions beyond their control. Don't push it. The ego is notoriously vulnerable. If you are tempted to dent it, you will put your cause back several steps. It is best to say just a little to open up a sensitive subject, then to give reassurance by snuggling up and going to sleep, rather than to hammer home your message all in one session. A responsive partner will think through what you have said and come up with their own ideas. A less responsive person may need the drip-drip technique. As long as you do it lightly and with care, avoiding a demanding edge to your voice or a needy whine, you should be able to get your relationship back on track.

fantasy stories

Sharing fantasies

Some couples like to share sexual fantasies in bed. In an atmosphere of complete trust and acceptance, this can be highly erotic. It can break down inhibitions and increase mental and physical intimacy. It can be fun in a teasing, imaginative way. Always be aware that it is a dream world that you are dealing with. If you get upset about your partner's fantasies, and use them to fuel an argument, you will have missed the point. A sexual fantasy differs from the real-life enactment of the very same scene because there is no responsibility involved. In the fantasy, everything runs in accordance with the fantasizer's wishes. The will of the other person or people do not intrude, nor do extraneous physical sensations. The fantasizer concentrates on marrying the fluid mental picture with the exquisite sensations of building up to orgasm.

If you think you might feel threatened by your partner's fantasies, then sharing them is not a good idea. Hearing that your partner entertains lustful thoughts about your best friend, or about someone at work, can make you angry and upset, unless you are confident that there is no desire to turn fantasy into reality. Start off if you like by exploring other people's fantasies – there are plenty of erotic books to help you get into the mood.

Sleeping easy

Whenever you go to bed with each other last thing at night, bear in mind the old maxim: 'Never let the sun go down on a quarrel'. We are not talking about deep and serious problems here, but everyday tiffs that if not resolved can smoulder away and grow to unreasonable proportions. Lying next to your lover, angry with something he or she has done or said that day, is not conducive to a refreshing night's sleep. Often a simple 'sorry' can break the tension and prompt an answer of 'I'm sorry too.'

privacy

Noises off

When a couple first meet and love is in the air, they can't wait to spend time alone together. In the early stages, both may be so impatient to get to know each other that time spent apart becomes meaningless, and work commitments, family and friends are neglected.

Of course, once the relationship is well established, things will necessarily begin to change. Familiarity and routine will take the edge off excitement. The birth of a baby will shift the whole focus of a relationship. All too quickly, time alone together becomes a rare event, and before the pair know it they may not even remember how to be alone together. The roles of householder and parent have swamped those of lover and confidant.

Children, grandparents, outside friends and interests, career worries, house, school and health problems can all widen the gap between them. But it don't have to be this way if a little thought is given to the changes that will inevitably occur with time. The key to keeping love alive is spending private time together, as often as you can.

Demands of children

Having a baby is a time of great joy, but also a time of great change. After all the drama of even the most easy of births, the couple will never be the same again. Their roles in life have changed. Their responsibilities have doubled and their privacy halved. If breastfeeding, those breasts that gave them both pleasure before now take on a new meaning and function. Some women find it very difficult to switch from being mother to lover, even when their bodies have recovered from the trauma of childbirth. Newborn babies are very demanding, feeding through the night is exhausting, but a new mother's attention has to be focused on the baby. Fathers, of course, are also affected. They too will be woken through the night. They might have worries about taking on their new financial responsibility. But above all, whereas before they were number one in their partner's life, now their physical and emotional needs usually come second.

Once the baby becomes a child, and there are, perhaps, additional babies in the family growing up, the demands on the parents' time and emotions are even greater. If thought has been put into adjusting to these changes, relationships can not only survive but grow closer. Just as when the parents were new lovers, privacy is of the essence.

Children brought up within the flexible constraints of a routine, and who have their own privacy respected as they get older, will respond to their parents' need for privacy. This is especially important where there are step-children living at home from a previous relationship. They are likely to have been through an emotional upheaval and resent their parent spending time with a new partner.

The children's bedtime, even if they are allowed to read or play quietly in their bedroom, should be at a regular time. They should be told that just as they have special times with their mother or their father, similarly this is their parents' special time together. Couples will benefit from spending at least part of this 'free' time exploring their relationship and keeping it alive. Talk about how you feel about each other and how you are getting on. What are the strengths and weaknesses of your partnership? It is all too easy to talk about nothing except the children and family plans, but save these discussions for another time.

Making time

Plan something special at least twice a month. Book a babysitter and go out for a meal. Go to the cinema, theatre or dancing, or whatever it was that you did together before the children were born. When babysitters are not available, plan a special evening in. Put off any visits from friends or relatives. Have a luxurious bath together followed by a sensual massage. If you like to read, read passages from something that you find erotic, or watch an erotic film. Ask personal questions about thoughts and needs, and insist on personal answers. In short, take time to devote yourselves to each other and rekindle the desire that brought you together in the first place.

are you both speaking

Most relationships that fail break down because of a lack of proper communication. You may be talking to each other, but do you really understand what your partner means? If we look up a word in a dictionary, the chances are that there will be at least two, if not more, definitions of that word. The definition we intend for a word or phrase should be clear from the context, but this is not always the case – tone and body language can alter the received meaning.

The gender divide

Just speaking the same language with your own sex has difficulties at times; differences in socio-economic backgrounds, expectations and needs can all lead to crossed wires. When a man and a women embark on communication, they have an additional hurdle in their different genders. Inevitably these have created differences in the way they were raised and in what society expects of them. In a committed relationship, both have to make an effort to understand and cross this divide, to reach a point where they are on the same wavelength.

Men often claim women are illogical, because most of their ways of looking at situations and talking about them are based on feelings. Men, on the other hand, may be accused of being unfeeling – viewing events and relationships in an overly logical way.

Women are raised to be loving and caring, and depend on their emotional instincts to pick up on any disharmony with their partner or within the family network. They will often express concern about someone's wellbeing, only to have the man in their life retort: 'Well, they look all right to me.' 'If it isn't broken, don't fix it' is a motto held firmly by many men, whereas women might detect a possible fracture and set about a preventative strategy. When this strategy goes wrong, and a situation deteriorates as a result, men will criticize women for interfering, or reading too much into something, and claim that it would have been wiser to leave well alone.

Female intuition is not renowned for glossing over issues women feel need to be addressed. Men who were once dependent on their mother's intuition to address their needs often complain that their partners kick up a fuss or become 'too emotional' over the slightest thing. But brushing worries under the carpet for the sake of carrying on as normal is not always a good idea. Men often suffer from stress related illnesses that could be avoided with a more open attitude to diagnosing and solving problems.

Perhaps one of the greatest differences between men and women is that most women do not compartmentalize their lives like most men tend to do. This may stem from the fact that women, especially those at home with children, have to attend to several tasks at once. They are constantly forced to 'switch hats'. Even working women with families who don't have the luxury of home help often admit to spending their lunch hour food-shopping or maybe making family dental or doctors' appointments.

Many men, on the other hand, are able to divorce their emotional life from their working life. One of the early reasons for discriminating against working women was their attention to family commitments. It was assumed they would have to take time off to look after sick children, and that even if they were not absent from work in body, they would still be absent in mind. That family commitments are not seen as a problem for working men has as much to do with the way men are taught to handle their emotions as with the social convention of women staying at home.

the same language ?

Failing to talk

The basic practical differences in the way men and women run their lives spill over into the way they communicate with each other. This becomes more apparent within a long-term relationship, when partners may have given up an early attempt at equal sharing and settled down into separate roles, often along traditional lines.

'Start as you mean to go on,' is not an easy maxim to follow in a relationship that is going to grow and develop as the individuals themselves change over the years. In a balanced partnership, new developments in views on anything from social issues to sexual needs should be discussed and where applicable assimilated. It is when they are ignored that real communication problems occur.

We all know of couples who barely speak to each other, just as we all know of those who are constantly at war, verbally and sometimes physically. Neither situation is healthy, although verbal warfare is perhaps preferable to silence, if only because there is a glimmer of a chance that one day what is being shouted will be heard.

Silence offers no such chance. Living with someone for any length of time does not automatically endow mind-reading ability. Men often complain, and sometimes women do too, that mind-reading is exactly what is expected. The classic comedy sketch in which one partner comes home to find the other obviously upset or fuming about something, asks what the matter is and receives a resounding 'Nothing!' is all too commonplace in real life.

If a relationship is to be emotionally fulfilling, grievances – no matter how small – must be aired, and the earlier the better before they grow out of proportion.

Raising issues

If an issue is discussed at the stage of disapproval or dislike, it stands a chance of being talked through – and heard – in a sensible, non-emotional way. It is not a good idea to suppress something purely because raising it is likely to hurt or cause an argument. A suppressed complaint affects the way we behave to our partner, and if it is suddenly released in a burst of temper, it is often accompanied by a host of other issues that are neither relevant nor perhaps even true. This does not make for an easy resolution.

Facing a difficult issue does not always mean dealing with something that is wrong with our relationship. The issue could be something that is likely to be beneficial to the relationship, but if it has never been discussed before, the thought of how our partner is going to respond can be quite daunting.

In a partnership, whatever is important or necessary to one partner must have an effect – albeit sometimes indirectly – on the other. Nowhere is this more significant than in the realms of sex. Women are reputedly becoming more assertive in their sexual demands, but there is still a long way to go. There still remain many barriers of social conditioning to be broken down.

A woman who has no qualms about making important decisions and taking action in most areas of her life may still balk at asking for a new aspect of sexual attention that she longs for, especially if her partner has never shown any desire in that direction. There is no place for faintheartedness or embarrassment in a loving bed. Who knows, once she has made the suggestion, she may find that her partner has been thinking along the same lines, but like her was fearful of mentioning it.

Trapped by the status quo

There is sometimes a feeling that two people have rubbed along together quite nicely without any major upheavals, so why rock the boat? If 'rubbing along together' is all that a couple want from a relationship, then why indeed.

Some people find change a challenge, a welcome stimulation in an everyday existence. Some people positively need to instigate change in order to keep going. Others hate it. They feel any change is an unquestionable nightmare to be avoided whenever possible. If your partner hates change and you are the one who wants to introduce a new element that will have a great effect on your relationship, you certainly have to work on your communication skills. And it will be worth it.

Communication breakdown case study

Not being able to say what we mean for fear of upsetting a partner, or simply because we are not very good at expressing ourselves, is all too common, even when partners have been together for years. Here is a fictitious example showing how stress and lack of confidence can cause communication problems in a relationship.

Jane is having a party. She has worked hard preparing the food and expects Peter, her lover of six months, to come over early to help her carry out furniture into the garden and fix up tree lights. Anxiety over the party's success gives her a sleepless night. In the early evening, she takes great care to make herself look as attractive as possible for Peter. She has planned an evening of Mexican food as a special treat for him.

Peter is not a person who enjoys parties, since he finds small talk and gossip futile. Moreover, there are one or two of Jane's friends whom he dislikes intensely. Adoring Jane, he fears disappointing her by not getting into the party mood. His boss keeps him late, leaving him no time to change out of his suit. He arrives at Jane's to find her friend, Steve, carrying out the chairs. Seeing him dressed inappropriately with time ticking on, Jane flies off the handle and says: 'You promised to be here at seven. How are you going to climb up the tree and fix the lights dressed like that?' Not wanting her to know that he has been working late to please his boss – his lack of assertiveness in the workplace has already been a bone of contention – Peter invents a visit to his mother as an excuse, adding pointedly: 'It doesn't look as if I'm needed anyway.' Jane is riled, as Peter sees too much of his mother for her liking – it was not a clever lie. What is more, he has failed to notice that she looks radiantly beautiful in her sexy dress.

The tree lights are a disaster as Peter does not know how to put them up. He thought he would be hanging storm lamps. The garden is on different levels and Jane is concerned about her guests' safety with wires trailing everywhere. She stresses this with a raised voice. Peter accuses her of being hysterical. To his humiliation, Steve takes over with Jane overly grateful at his side. Peter tells Jane he is going home to change, to which she retorts furiously: 'Don't bother to come back,' and turns her back on him to hide the hot tears welling in her eyes. Peter storms off, feeling angry, useless and rejected.

The argument evolves through a lack of communication. Instead of talking about how bad they both feel and helping each other, Jane and Peter quickly let the situation get out of control.

Jane fails to communicate:

The type of lighting she expects Peter to fix up.

• The fact that she is not having fun but is tired and anxious about the success of the party.

• The fact that she believes Peter cares more about his mother than about her, which is why he has arrived late.

• The fact that she is hurt by his lack of compliments.

• The fact that she in no way finds her friend Steve more attractive than Peter.

• The fact that she really wants Peter to be with her at the party, and to stay the night.

Peter fails to communicate:

• The real reason for his being late.

• The fact that he thinks Jane looks terrific.

• The fact that he knows nothing and cares even less about garden lights.

• The fact that Steve makes him feel insecure and jealous.

• The fact that he wants Jane to beg him to stay at the party.

How much happier it would have been if Peter had explained his real reasons for being late and had complimented Jane on her appearance instead of just apologizing for his own. If he had owned up to his lack of DIY skills and been quite contented for another man to do the honours, he would have been able to help Jane in a more important way, by listening to how stressed she was and soothing her stretched nerves. Unfortunately, we can't always think of the right things to say until after the event.

Jane should have talked to Peter about whether he would enjoy the party and how he would feel about meeting people he does not like. And at some stage soon they should address the more important issue of Peter's mother.

It is easy to see from the outside how things start to go wrong and accelerate downhill. In our own relationships, where objectivity is hard to grasp, we are not so gifted. Taking time to listen and asking relevant questions, being aware that even important needs may be expressed in veiled terms and trying not to jump to conclusions are some of the ways in which communication can be improved.

6: raising sexua

awareness

This chapter presents a range of everyday exercises to promote your physical and mental wellbeing in general and for enhancing your sexuality in particular. You can practise these exercises either alone or with your lover. The Alexander Technique gives you greater poise, and heightens grace and confidence. Yoga exercises allow you to free your mind of everyday clutter while making your body supple and keeping it youthful. Meditation calms and refreshes the spirit and awakens the senses. Finally, Tantric exercises increase your sexual power and make love last longer.

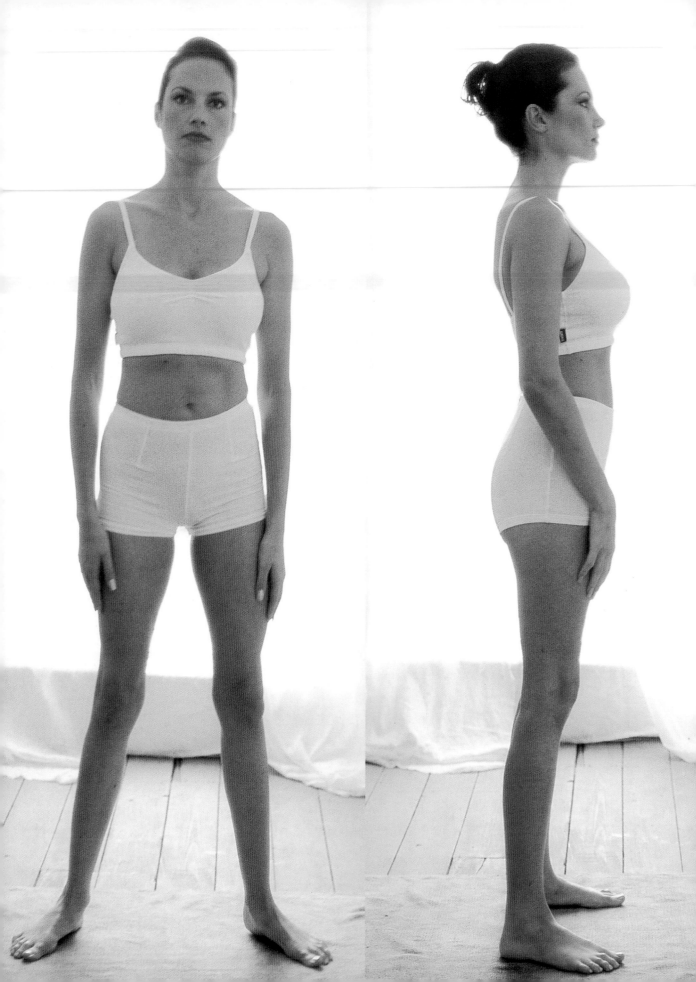

the alexander technique

The Alexander Technique

Being at ease with your body is important for good sex. The way we hold ourselves, stand, sit and move reflects how we see ourselves and how we interact with the world. A posture that is upright but relaxed, and movements that are smooth and unhurried, reveal a person unselfconsciously at one with their body. As you read this, are you attempting to straighten your back or push back your shoulders? Are you aware that you slump or slouch?

Watch a young child at play and you will see a natural grace and poise that most adults have lost. Throughout our lives, we subject our bodies to repeated physical and mental tensions that slowly build an invisible straitjacket around us. From our schooldays, we spend too many hours sitting at a desk that is the wrong height. We then graduate to bigger wrong-height desks, or to a lifetime of bending and lifting, or of performing other repetitive actions that torture our bodies gradually over the years until the tension manifests itself as illness, such as headaches, backaches or depression. Our body is our most valuable asset, yet most of us take only cosmetic care of it until it is too late.

The Alexander Technique aims to teach people how to unlearn habitual misuse of the body and to return to the natural poise and grace of early childhood. Alexander Technique followers experience a new-found freedom from physical stress and a sense of mental and emotional wellbeing – both fundamental to a fulfilling sex life.

The Alexander Technique was developed by an Australian, Frederick Alexander, during the first half of the 20th century. Alexander made his living giving theatrical recitals but was thwarted by health problems, in particular by breathing difficulties that he first developed in childhood and which caused him to lose his voice. The medical profession washed their hands of him, so he devoted his time to curing himself. He spent long hours in front of the mirror, watching the way he used his body. After many years of study and self-training, he learned to correct minute but crucial faults of posture and bearing, and his breathing problem disappeared. He returned to his theatrical career, but became internationally known for his successful teaching of the Alexander Technique.

The Alexander Technique is best practised with the help of a properly trained teacher who can spot imbalances in the way you stand, sit and move. Remember, it took Alexander years to discover his own postural weaknesses. However, there are many exercises that you can try at home.

How do you stand?

Your aim is to stand in a balanced way. Unbalanced posture puts a strain on the entire skeletal system as well as on the internal organs. Stand with bare feet in your normal position in front of a mirror and ask yourself these questions:

Am I leaning over to one side, or am I balanced on both of my legs? Shift your weight from one leg to the other and back again to help you decide.

Am I leaning forwards or backwards, or am I standing straight? Feel how your feet are contacting the ground. Do you feel more pressure on the ball of the foot, or on the heel, or are you evenly balanced between them? Many people stand leaning back from the waist with head and shoulders thrust forwards. This causes fatigue and bad internal pressures, as does standing with shoulders hunched and head slumped forwards.

Am I standing on the inside or the outside of my feet? Look in the mirror to see how your lower legs and knees are aligned. Are your feet pushing them outwards or inwards? You may be doing one thing on one side and the other thing on the other side. Another way of checking this is to look at your shoes. Do the heels wear out evenly? Are they trodden over to one side?

How do you sit?

Many of us spend a large amount of our time seated, and an unbalanced posture can lead to aches and pains as well as internal disorders. Sit as you normally do, but sideways on to a mirror, and ask yourself these questions:

Am I sitting squarely, or do I lean to one side? Note that crossing your legs will create an imbalance of the spine.

Am I slumped forwards with shoulders hunched, or do I sit in a rigid upright position with my back hollowed and chest thrust forwards? A well balanced position in between the two is best for your well-being.

Where are my feet? They should be squarely on the floor, giving balance to your spine.

Am I leaning against the back of the chair? You should be sitting in the position that is right for your body, not using the chair as a support.

How do you walk?

Most of us spend far too much energy while walking, by creating unnecessary tension. Try the following:

Let your head lead and your body will follow.

Work with gravity rather than against it.

Try not to displace your weight to the side when taking a step forwards.

When you take a step, do not initiate the movement by lifting your thigh. This is a waste of energy. Allow yourself to fall forwards, then save yourself from falling by taking a step.

Balance your weight evenly on your foot as it comes to rest on the ground.

Make sure that your feet point straight ahead, not in or out, as they touch the ground.

Concentrate on observing imbalance rather than striving to correct it. If you make a conscious effort to correct every movement, you may find that you over-compensate. By remaining aware of postural imbalance, you will slowly acquire a natural balance.

1

2

3

yoga

4

Yoga

Yoga is the world's most ancient system of personal development. The word *yoga* means 'joining' – the joining of the body and the consciousness to an unchanging reality that lies beyond. It is a process that enables the shedding of personal preoccupations and the clutter of everyday life. Yoga strengthens and tones the body, improving the functioning of muscles and joints. The spine becomes more flexible and the exercises also work on the internal organs, the glands and the nerves. You will find that the physical and emotional effects of yoga allow you to tune in to your body's deepest sexual feelings.

It is difficult to get in touch with your partner when one or the other of you is distracted and tense. You both need to be centred – in touch with yourselves – before you can connect with each other. Yoga can help, because it enables you to relax. It is possible to be tense all the time without realizing, even to lie rigidly in bed, grimly awaiting sleep, without realizing that mind and body are merely galvanized for the sound of the alarm clock and the next headlong rush into action. Try consciously tensing and relaxing your muscles to see just how keyed up you are.

Physical relaxation brings a feeling of wellbeing, as well as freedom from aches and pains, but yoga gives more than this. As you continue to practise it, yoga brings a sense of the harmony and peace of mind that are the prerequisites of true self-knowledge. Yoga provides a touchstone of relaxation and stillness that will always enable you to get your bearings in the confusion of everyday life.

The exercise of yoga consists of getting into and out of a series of postures, or *asanas*. The movements are slow and graceful, never jerky. They extend your reach gradually and should not be forced. After a yoga session, you should feel relaxed and full of energy, not exhausted and strained. Breathing is especially important to help you move correctly.

In performing the following sequence of 12 *asanas*, do not worry if you cannot get into some of the positions at first.

You will be able to achieve them in time as you become more supple. Imagine yourself forming the shapes in the photographs, even if you cannot actually achieve them.

As its name – the sun salutation – suggests, this series of twelve *asanas* is traditionally performed at dawn, as a greeting to the sun. However, it is also an ideal exercise sequence that you and your partner can perform together to rid yourself of the tensions of the day before you go to bed.

The sun salutation

Each bend or stretch in this series of exercises balances the one before, improving the flexibility of your spine and the suppleness of the muscles.

1   Stand with your back straight and your feet together. Press your palms together in the prayer position. Feel balanced. Exhale.

2   Inhale and stretch up your arms, arching your back from the waist and pressing your hips forwards. Keep your legs straight and let your neck relax.

3   Exhale and bring your body forwards and down so that your hands touch the floor. In time, you should be able to press your palms alongside your feet.

4   Inhale and push one leg out behind you, touching the floor with the balls of your toes and your knee. Stretch your leg and arch your back. Lift your chin to form a continuous curve.

5   Holding your breath, stretch the second leg back to join the first. Raise yourself up on your hands and feet. Keep your legs, back and neck in a straight line, looking down between your hands.

6   Exhale, lowering yourself to the ground – first the knees, then the chest and finally the forehead. Keep your toes curled and your hips raised.

The sun salutation continued

7   Inhale, lowering your hips to the ground and raising your torso. Point your toes away from you and completely arch your back.

8   Exhale, raising your hips, curling your toes under and bending your head inwards. Be conscious of making a regular inverted 'V' shape.

9   Inhale, stepping forwards with one foot between your palms. This position is the mirror image of step 4.

10 Exhale, bringing the second leg forwards to join the first, as in step 3.

11 Inhale, lifting your torso up and stretching your arms forwards, then back over your head, as in step 2.

12 Exhale, returning to an upright position. Let your arms fall gently to your sides.

meditation

Our minds are constantly spinning, planning and worrying about the future, analysing and agonizing about the past. We spend much more time in yesterday and tomorrow than we do in the here and now, and this is a major cause of relationship breakdown, as well as of stress and illness.

Making love is the best way there is of emptying the mind, giving in to sensation and existing intensely in the present. Meditation is another way of doing this. It frees your head of thought, of the critical processes that get in the way of spontaneous feeling. It lets you 'go with the flow'. It makes you alert yet relaxed. If stress gets in the way of making love, learning to meditate can bring you back to that blissful floating state in which sex comes naturally.

The techniques for meditation are unbelievably simple, but because it is often so difficult to empty the mind of thought, meditation needs a lot of practice. You may find that you achieve something similar to a meditative state through another activity, such as gardening or swimming, that involves feeling and dreaming or intuition rather than thinking.

How to begin

Let yourself come down first from the rush of the busy day. Begin by ordering and calming the outside: take a shower, do the washing-up, pick up clothes you left lying on the floor. It is important to create a soothing environment. Flowers and plants help, as do soft lights or candles. If you would like to meditate to music, choose something without words, and preferably music such as baroque or New Age music, or music from the world of nature, such as whalesong or birdsong.

Some people like to start by cleansing their aura. The aura is the energy field that surrounds each one of us, and which shows up in Kirlian photography. Cleanse it by stroking your body in firm lines from top to bottom, using the third and fourth fingers of each hand alternately. Start at the bridge of the nose, the 'third eye'. Work over the crown of the head, down the neck and down the spine as far as you can. Pick up the line with the fingers of your other hand and continue it right down the spine and down one leg. Repeat for the other side. Repeat for each arm, and then for the front of the body, down the centre, past the pubis and along the inside of the legs. As you reach the end of the line each time, give your hand a shake to get rid of the blocked energy and make way for new energy to flow in.

Now choose a comfortable posture. The important thing here is to allow the body to feel both balanced and well grounded. Yoga practitioners prefer the lotus position, but if you cannot manage this with ease, you could sit cross-legged, or upright on a chair with your feet on the ground and hands on your knees. The easiest position of all is the corpse position. Lie flat on your back on a firm surface with your legs slightly parted and your feet falling naturally out-wards. Stretch your arms out at 45 degrees from your body with palms relaxed and facing up.

Techniques

Now choose your meditation technique from the following:

Breathe Close your eyes. Breathe normally. After each exhalation, count silently, until you reach ten exhalations. Count again from the beginning until you reach ten again. Carry on doing this, starting at one every time you are distracted by your mind butting in with an annoying train of thought.

Listen Close your eyes and listen, to a tape or to the silence, or to distant noises from elsewhere in your home or from the street. Just be passive and listen, without analysing, explaining or judging the sounds that you hear. Shut off the critical function of your mind and accept.

Look Use your eyes afresh. Let them wander gently over everything you can see. Let the colours and shapes exist for themselves without mentally putting them into words. Experience the sensation of seeing without thinking.

Gaze Choose an object to contemplate – perhaps a favourite stone from the beach, a candle or a flower. Set it at a comfortable distance in front of you. Let your eyes get lost in this object and empty your mind of thought. As thoughts try to impinge, invite the object to soak them up and blot them out. Let your eyes slide out of focus and keep a steady, unblinking gaze.

Speak Choose a mantra – a word or phrase that you can repeat over and over again. Many people like to use a homemade word with a satisfying sound – the meaning is unimportant. As you repeat the word, feel it resonate in your lower belly. Give yourself over to the sound vibrations to free yourself of thought.

Feel This is best done lying down. Concentrate on being inside your body and on feeling each part of it in turn. Do not move any part of your body, but just be aware of its shape and position from the inside out. Start with your toes and work up, slowly, to the top of your head. This is also an excellent way of relaxing.

meditation

tantric sex

Tantric sex

Tantra comes from two ancient Sanskrit words meaning expansion and liberation. It is a form of Buddhist and Hindu teaching that sees sex as a way of expanding and exploring spirituality. In Tantra, you use each of the five senses to the limit, and anything that gives you and your partner pleasure is good. The idea is that by involving your whole being in a sexual union without guilt, pleasure turns to bliss and energizes the whole of your life, bringing radiance and healing. Sexual energy, as many people can testify, has the power to transform your life, make you happy and give you confidence and self-esteem.

Tantra is a philosophy of wholeness and oneness in which the man is advised to explore his feminine side and the woman to explore her masculine qualities. Both partners are encouraged to keep physically aware and healthy, and to meditate together. In the achievement-oriented West, orgasm is seen as the goal of sex, particularly by men. In Tantra, female satisfaction and orgasm are very important, but male orgasm should be delayed so that bliss can be prolonged. The journey is all, and after arrival, the journey is over. Men get exhausted by ejaculation, so Tantrists learn to orgasm without ejaculating. Men who practise Tantric sex can have multiple orgasms and whole-body orgasms like women.

Techniques

There are several ways a man can make his erection subside and delay ejaculation:

- Stay completely still, relax the genital and anal muscles and press your tongue against the roof of your mouth just behind your teeth.

- Stay still and take deep, regular breaths.

- Withdraw your penis a little until the urgency passes, then alternate nine shallow thrusts with one deeper one.

- Press the index finger and thumb on your perineum, midway between the anus and scrotum. Either you or your partner can do this.

- Use the squeeze technique developed by the sexologists Masters and Johnson. Place the thumb on the frenulum, on the underside of the penis, with the index and middle fingers on the ridge of the glans penis on the upper side, and squeeze for 10–15 seconds. Again, either you or your partner can do this.

index

A

abdomen massage 105
abuse 12
AIDS 65
Alexander Technique 127, 129
allergies treatment 96
almond oil 24, 57
aphrodisiacs 31, 41–9, 58, 68, 99
aquatherapy 108–9
Arab customs 55
arm massage 104–5
aroma, see smell
aromatherapy 51, 54–9, 108–9
arousal 15, 21–5, 32, 35–6, 39, 51–9, 70, 126–41
artichokes, stuffed 45
asanas, Yoga 132–5
asparagus souffle 46–7
attraction 12, 17
aubergines, the Imam fainted 47
awareness raising 126–41
Ayurveda 55

B

back massage 102–3
basil oil 58
bathing 22, 35, 57, 86–7, 100, 108–9, 113
bed 113, 114–5
beef chilli 42
benzoin oil 58
bergamot oil 58, 101
blue movies 26
body language 11, 15, 17, 120
bonding 34, 66
breathing 57, 58, 100, 129, 138
breakdown case study 123–5
buttocks massage 103

C

camomile oil 101
candles 15, 35, 57, 68, 99
cardamom coffee 49
caressing 34–5, 39, 78
cedarwood oil 58, 101
censers 55
chamomile oil 58
chest massage 105
children 22, 66, 116, 119
chilli 42
Chinese customs 32, 49, 55, 95
chocolate, Mexican hot 49
cinnamon oil 101
clary sage oil 58
clitoris stimulation 24, 25, 39, 79, 109
clove oil 58
cobra position 84
coffee, cardamom 49
communication 17, 36, 60–2, 66, 110–25
companionship 66
condoms 65
congestion release 95–7
contraception 65
corpse position, Yoga 137
cuissade position 81
cunnilingus 39
cunnilingus position 79
cypress oil 58

D

deer position 74–5
disease, see illness
dress 9, 19, 21, 29

E

effleurage massage 100, 102–6
Egyptian customs 32, 95
ejaculation delay 141
essential oils 55, 58–9, 68, 99, 100, 108–9
eucalyptus oil 57, 58
exercises 127–37
excitement see arousal
eye contact 15, 17

F

facial hair 32
families 22, 66, 116, 119
fantasies 29, 114
feeling meditation technique 138
feet massage 106–7
fellatio 39, 78
female position control 84–5
fidelity 66
figs, lamb with honey 45
foods 31, 32, 41–9
foreplay 34–5, 108–9
frankincense 58, 101
frenulum 25, 39, 141
fruit, pasta with 46

G

galbanium oil 58
gamahuche 39
gazing meditation technique 138
gender characteristics 19, 29, 62, 120
genital stimulation 24
geranium oil 58, 101
ginger, sole with oysters 44

H

hands massage 104–5
health aspects 55, 57–9, 64–6, 90–7
herbs, pasta with fruit 46
HIV 65
honey, lamb with figs 45
hormones 62, 99
hot beef chilli 42
hygiene 25, 32, 36

I

illness 36, 62, 65, 66, 120
Imam fainted, the 47
Indian customs 55, 99
infection release 95–7
inhibitions 29, 36, 113
insomnia relief 59

J-K

jasmine oil 58
juniper oil 58, 101

Kirlian philosophy 137–8
kissing 17, 31–5, 39, 78
kneading massage 100–3, 106

L

labia stimulation 24
lady's will position 75
lamb with honey and figs 45
lavender oil 59, 101
legs massage 106–7

142

lemon oil 59
lemon syllabub 48
lemon grass oil 59
libido 66, 68
licking 31, 35, 39, 78
limbic area of the brain 53
limes, orange sorbet 49
lingam position 78
lip care 32
listening 62, 113, 125, 138
looking technique 138
lotus position, Yoga 137
love at first sight 9, 11
lubricants 24, 25, 39

M

mandarin ducks position 84
marjoram oil 59
massage 31, 57, 62, 90–3, 99–109
masturbation 24–5, 89
meditation 137–8
menstrual pain relief 58, 93
meridians for shiatsu 90–3
Mexican hot chocolate 49
mirror image position 70
mirrors 26
missionary position 77
Moroccan customs 99
mouth massage 31
mussels in white wine 44–5
myrrh 59

N

nakedness 21–2
neroli oil 59, 101
nibbling 31, 35
nipple stimulation 35, 109
nudist camps 22
nuzzling 39, 62

O

oils 24, 35, 57–9, 99, 101, 108–9
ointments 57
olfactory nerves 53, 55
oral contact 32
oral sex 31, 34–9
oral sex positions 78–9
orange and lime sorbet 49
orange oil 59
orgasm delay 75
orgasm stimulation 24, 25, 39, 114

ovaries treatment 95–6
oysters, sole with ginger 44

P

pain relief, shiatsu 92–3
Palm beach giant prawns 42
partnership 120–1
pasta with fruit 46
patchouli 59, 68, 101, 109
peas, risi e bisi 46
penis 25, 39
penis capture 72
penis penetration simulation 39
penis stimulation 109
penis withdrawal 141
peppermint oil 57, 59
perfume, see smell
perineum 25, 141
petrissage massage 100, 104–6
pheromones 51, 53
pine oil 59
pornography 26, 68
positions 36, 79–89
posture 129–30
prawns, Palm Beach 42
pregnancy, safe position 84
pressing position 82–3
pressure points
   reflexology 95–7
   shiatsu 90–3
privacy 26, 99, 116, 119
problems, overcoming 113, 115,
   121, 123–5
prostate stimulation 25
prostate treatment 95–6
pubic hair 25, 29, 39

R

receptor nerves 53, 55
recipes 42–9
reflexology 94–7
relaxation techniques 132–8
risi e bisi 46
room scents 57
rose oil 59, 101
rosemary oil 59, 101
rosewood oil 59

S

sandalwood oil 59, 68, 109
scent, see smell

semen 39, 65
sensitive areas 35, 39
sex aids 24
sex drive 66–89
shiatsu 90–3
shoes 29
showers 22
sitting 130
smell 32, 35, 36, 50–9, 68, 109
smoking 32
sole with oysters 44
soporifics 49
speaking meditation technique 138
spoons position 84
standing 129
standing positions 80–1, 83
strawberry fizz 48–9
stress problems 62, 99, 120
stuffed artichokes 45
sucking 31, 32, 39, 78
sun salutation 132–5

T

tangerine oil 59
Tantric sex 6, 141
Tapotement massage 100
tea tree oil 59
tension relief 55, 57, 59, 95–7, 99,
   129
tequila 49
testicles treatment 95–6
thyme oil 59
togetherness 62, 113, 116, 119
tongue movements 32, 34–5, 39
touching 17, 21–2, 60–2, 99
towels 99, 109, 113
trust 29, 36
tsubos 92–3

U–Z

undressing 21–2
uterus treatment 95–6
vagina, stimulation 25, 39
vagina penetration simulation 39
voyeurism 26
vulva stimulation 25, 70
walking 131
watching sex 26
yawning position 82–3
ylang ylang 59, 68, 101, 109
Yoga 127, 132–8
zones for reflexology 95–7

Publishing Director Alison Goff

Executive Editor Jane McIntosh

Project Editor Katey Day

Creative Director Keith Martin

Design Manager Bryan Dunn

Senior Designer David Godfrey

Special Photography Colin Gotts

Models Nicole Bouchet at Supermodel and
Darren Paul at Verve Model Management

Picture Researchers Christine Junemann
and Rosie Garai

Production Controller Lisa Moore

acknowledgments